I0016875

Hacking Discrete Math With Python 3

Isabella Romeo

Sherwood Forest

http://CalculusCastle.com

Hacking Discrete Math With Python 3, Zeroth Edition, by Bella Reomeo
Last Revised on: 5/27/18 (Version 0.1.1049)
Sherwood Forest Books, Los Angeles, CA, USA
ISBN-13: 978-1720405979
ISBN-10: 1720405972

© 2018 B. E. Shapiro. All Rights Reserved. No part of this document may be reproduced, stored electronically, or transmitted by any means without prior written permission of the author.

THIS DOCUMENT IS PROVIDED IN THE HOPE THAT IT WILL BE USEFUL BUT WITHOUT ANY WARRANTY, WITHOUT EVEN THE IMPLIED WARRANTY OF MERCHANTABILITY OR FITNESS FOR A PARTICULAR PURPOSE. THE DOCUMENT IS PROVIDED ON AN "AS IS" BASIS AND THE AUTHOR HAS NO OBLIGATIONS TO PROVIDE CORRECTIONS OR MODIFICATIONS. THE AUTHOR MAKES NO CLAIMS AS TO THE ACCURACY OF THIS DOCUMENT. IN NO EVENT SHALL THE AUTHOR BE LIABLE TO ANY PARTY FOR DIRECT, INDIRECT, SPECIAL, INCIDENTAL, OR CONSEQUENTIAL DAMAGES, INCLUDING LOST PROFITS, UNSATISFACTORY CLASS PERFORMANCE, POOR GRADES, CONFUSION, MISUNDERSTANDING, EMOTIONAL DISTURBANCE OR OTHER GENERAL MALAISE ARISING OUT OF THE USE OF THIS DOCUMENT OR ANY SOFTWARE DESCRIBED HEREIN, EVEN IF THE AUTHOR HAS BEEN ADVISED OF THE POSSIBILITY OF SUCH DAMAGE. IT MAY CONTAIN TYPOGRAPHICAL ERRORS. WHILE NO FACTUAL ERRORS ARE INTENDED THERE IS NO SURETY OF THEIR ABSENCE.

First editions suck. Especially ones without editors. Don't expect this one to be any better. Please report any errors, omissions, or suggestions for improvements through the form at
https://github.com/bellaromeo/discrete-math-book/issues.

The only authorized distributor of the electronic version of this book is Gumroad. If you have obtained an electronic copy from any other source your copy is unauthorized and in violation of international copyright law.

This is a draft with (probably) lots of typos in it. Please report errors!

Table of Contents

Preface

This book contains lecture notes for an *elementary* one semester class in discrete math (DM) for computer science and computer engineering students. If you've come this far, then chances are you're already familiar with the $300 textbooks that rule the roost (and strain the muscles). I call these the big box books (BBBs). I use these notes to help students navigate a pathway through the BBBs, and then throw in a modicum of Python. In my experience, students relate better to this material when it is presented in the context of programming. Python is used as an exemplar because it is generic, easy to learn, and free (as in both beer and speech). While a small number of mathematical exercises have been included, I have relegated the task of enumerating huge reams of exercises to the BBBs.

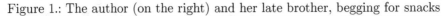

Figure 1.: The author (on the right) and her late brother, begging for snacks

As this book is still mostly in draft and I lack a coherent editor (as well as opposable thumbs), there are lots of typographical errors. I would appreciate the reporting of errors to `https://github.com/bellaromeo/discrete-math-book/issues` so my human can fix them. I welcome and encourage suggestions for additional content and exercises. I thank you for buying this book so my human can buy me more kibble.

Table of Symbols Used

$A \land B$	A and B
$A \lor B$	A or B
$A \Rightarrow B$	If A then B, A implies B, A is sufficient for B
$A \Leftrightarrow B$	A if and only if B, A is necessary and sufficient for B
$\neg P$	Negation, not P
$\therefore P$	Therefore P
$A \oplus B$	B xor B, exclusive or
$P \equiv Q$	P is quivalent to Q
$\forall x$	For all x, for every x, for each x
$\exists y$	There exists a y
$x \in S$	Is an element of, x is an element of S
$A \cup B$	Set union
$A \cap B$	Set intersection
$A - B$	Set difference
$A \times B$	Cartesian product of A and B
$\emptyset$	Empty set
$\mathbb{N}$	The natural numbers (nonnegative integers)
$\mathbb{R}$	The real numbers
$\mathbb{U}$	The universal set
$\mathbb{Z}^+$	The positive numbers
$\mathbb{Z}$	The integers
$\square$	QED, *quod erat demonstrandum*, placed at the end of a proof
$\rightarrow$	Production arrow, the operations on the left produces the result on the right
$\mathbf{x} \leftarrow \mathbf{y}$	The value $\mathbf{y}$ is associated with memory location $\mathbf{x}$
Σ	Alphabet (of characters or symbols)
Σ^*	Strings over Σ
Σ^n	Strings of length n over Σ
Σ^+	Strings of length at least 1 over Σ

1. Logic and Truth Tables

Mathematical **statements**, or **propositions**, represent declarative sentences in English (or other spoken languages) but are more precise. To be completely clear when we state a proposition, we will build our statements from the following words, or **logical connectives**: "**and**," "**or**," and "**not**." From time to time, we may add other special words to our vocabulary, such as "**if**," "**then**," "**implies**" or "**iff**." We will assign special meanings to these words; their meanings are more precise than the meanings that are typically used in conversational language. We will assign a **truth value**, either "**True**" or "**False**," to each statement. The truth value is determined by the logical connectives and values of the **variables** (nouns) in the sentence. For example,

24 is divisible by 6 **and** 24 is divisble by 2

if (x is even) **then** (x is divisible by 2)

if (y is an integer) **then** ((y is even) **or** (y is odd)

For simplicity we will often label a statement.

P: The square root of 4 is 7.

Q: The square root of 9 is 3.

Even though P is **False**, it is still a valid statement. Q is a **True** statement, and it is also valid statement, as is the statment R:

R: P **or** Q

Operations such as **or**, **and**, and **not** can be used to join both variables and other statements. We can nest parenthesis to make the meaning more clear.

The **or** operation is used to indicate that a statement is true when either one or both of a pair of variables is **True**. We can describe the process by

---

exhaustively tabulating all the possible combinations of X and Y as tuples: (**True**, **True**), (**True**, **False**), (**False**, **True**), and (**False**, **False**), and then giving the result of X **or** Y in a third column or third element of the tuples. The result is called a **truth table**. It is common to shorten the values listed in a truth table from **True** and **False** to simply T and F to save space.

Definition 1.1. Disjunction, The or Operator.

We define the **or** operator as follows: X **or** Y is **True** if either (or both) of the following are **True**:
1. $X =$ **True**
2. $Y =$ **True**

If neither of the above cases holds, then X **or** Y is said to be **False**. We may also write X **or** Y symbolically as $X \vee Y$.

X	Y	$X \vee Y$
True	True	True
True	False	True
False	True	True
False	False	False

The expression $X \vee Y$ is sometimes called the **disjunction** of X and Y, but we will not use that term here. .

Operations such as **or** and **and** may be expressed in either a prefix notation, e.g.,

$$\mathbf{or}(A,B)$$

or with an infix notation,

$$\mathbf{and}(P,Q)$$

For these operations the prefix operation is potentially much more general (once we define what the mean) because they can be extended to operate on more variables:

$$\mathbf{or}(A,B,C,...)$$

We cannot define multi-variable (greater than 2) operator functions at this

---

time because we do not yet know how to nest the parenthesis properly (we will see how to do this in chapter 2 for **and** and **or**). The **not** (or negation) operation is only defined with a prefix version. Many computer languages implement both versions.

The **and** connective is used to indicate that a statement is true when both of a pair of variables are **True**. If either one or both of the variables are **False**, the statement is **False**.

Definition 1.2. Conjunction, The AND Operator

We define the **and** operator as follows: X **and** Y is **True** if both of the following are **True**:
    1. $X =$ **True**; and
    2. $Y =$ **True**
If either one (or both) of the above cases does not occur, then X **and** Y is said to be **False**. We may also write X **and** Y symbolically as $X \wedge Y$.

X	Y	$X \wedge Y$
True	True	True
True	False	False
False	True	False
False	False	False

The expression $X \wedge Y$ is sometimes called the **conjunction** of X and Y, but we will not use that term here.

The **not** (negation) is used to switch a variable on or off. If the value of a variable is **True**, then **not** X is **False**, and if X is **False**, then **not** X is **True**. We may write **not** X symbolically as $\sim X$ or $\neg X$ (both notations are in common use). The truth table for a negation is

X	$\neg X$
True	False
False	True

We define the **conditional** notation to handle statements of the form **if** P **then** Q. We will use the term **implies**, rather than **conditional**, for this type of notation, and, for the most part, and say P **implies** Q rather than **if** P **then** Q. Actually, a special symbol for **implies** is not necessary, but

---

we will find it very convenient. This is because **if... then...** statements can always be expressed in terms of a combination of **or** and **not**.

Definition 1.3. Implication

We say P **implies** Q is **True**, and write $P \Rightarrow Q$, when the statement $\neg P \vee Q$ is **True**. $P \Rightarrow Q$ is sometimes stated as **if** P **then** Q. The left hand side (P) is sometimes called the **premise** of the implication, and we say that P is **sufficient** to prove Q. The right hand side (Q) is sometimes called the **conclusion**, and we say that Q is **necessary** for P. The truth table for $P \Rightarrow Q$ is:

P	Q	$P \Rightarrow Q$
T	T	T
T	F	F
F	T	T
F	F	T

The only way that $P \Rightarrow Q$ can ever be **False** is if P is **True** and Q is **False**. An example would be this:

P: Some dogs have short hair   (**True**)
Q: All dogs have long hair   (**False**)
$P \Rightarrow Q$ (**False**)

Here the premise is **True** and the conclusion is **False**, so the implication is **False**. If the conclusion is **True**, the implication is always **True**, regardless of the premise. If both the premise and the conclusion are **False**, we have no evidence with which to dispute the truth of the implication, so we say that the implication is (vacuously) **True**. This gives us the same truth table as $\neg P \vee Q$, which explains why we take this as the definition of the implication.

If P is both necessary and sufficient for Q then we have both $P \Rightarrow Q$ and $Q \Rightarrow P$. We write this symbolically as $P \Leftrightarrow Q$, and say that P is true if and only if Q is true.

Definition 1.4. If and Only If

We say P **if and only if** Q, and write P **iff** Q, or $P \Leftrightarrow Q$, if

$$(P \Rightarrow Q) \wedge (Q \Rightarrow P)$$

The expression $P \Leftrightarrow Q$ is sometimes called a **biconditional**. We call $P \Rightarrow Q$ the **sufficiency** (because P is sufficient to prove Q) an dwe call $Q \Rightarrow P$ the **necessity** (because Q is necessary for P to be true in the expression $P \Rightarrow Q$). We also say that P is both **necessary** and **sufficient** for Q (and vice-versa, which makes the definitions of necessity and sufficiency ambiguous).

We construct the truth table for $P \Leftrightarrow Q$ here.

P	Q	$P \Rightarrow Q$	$Q \Rightarrow P$	$P \Leftrightarrow Q$
T	T	T	T	T
T	F	F	T	F
F	T	T	F	F
F	F	T	T	T

With a little work (exercise 1), we can show that the truth value of $P \Leftrightarrow Q$ is the same as the truth value of $(P \wedge Q) \vee (\neg P \wedge \neg Q)$. Thus the symbol $\Leftrightarrow$ is actually redundant; however, it is kept around for convenience.

If there are n distinct variables in a statement, then there are 2^n different ways they can be combined to form a truth table. This gives the number of lines in a truth table. A statement with two variables will have a truth table with four lines; a statement with three variables will have a truth table with eight lines; a statement with four variables with have a truth table with 16 lines; and so forth.

Similarly, there are precisely four ways that we can pair the values **True** and **False**: (T,T), (T,F), (F,T), and (F,F). Thus there are 16 ways we can define a function $f(x, y)$, since the value of $f(x, y)$ can be either T or F. We have defined four of these: **and** ($f(x, y) = x \wedge y$); **or** ($f(x, y) = x \vee y$); **implies** ($f(x, y) = x \Rightarrow y$); and **iff** ($f(x, y) = x \Leftrightarrow y$). There are two additional constant functions $f(x, y) = T$ and $f(x, y) = F$ (the result is always **True** or always **False**, regardless of the input. This leaves ten other functions that we have left unnamed. In general, we do not have to define all 16 of these functions because they can all be reproduced from the standard named functions. Some of these are useful in spopsecific disciplines, such as computer architecture. Examples are the **XOR** (exclusive or), **NAND** (**not and**), **NOR** (**not or**), and **XNOR** (exclusive not or) (exercise 4).

We may combine operations in an expression in any order to form more complicated expressions. To indicate which operations are to be performed first, we can use parenthesis. After that, operations are evaluated from left to right in the following order:

Priority	Operation	
0	()	highest priority
1	$\neg$	
2	$\wedge$, $\vee$	equal priority
3	$\Rightarrow$, $\Leftrightarrow$	equal priority

Boolean Variables in Python

Python boolean variables can take on two values, **True** and **False**. All Python expressions have a truth value.

```
x=1
y=2
z=x<y
z
```

```
True
```

All other Python variables can be tested for truth but will be evaluated as **True**, with the following exceptions, which will always be evaluated as **False**: a zero integer, decimal or fraction; a zero length sequence type such as **[]**, **[]**, **{}**; a null string; or the constants **None** or **False**. A Python variable can be tested for its truth value directly; it is not usually necessary to use "**== True**" in a test:

```
if z==True:
    print(x,"<",y)
```

```
1<2
```

```
if z:
    print(x,"<",y)
```

```
1<2
```

Python has three boolean operations: **and**, **or**, and **not**; these implement the operations of the same name that we have described earlier in this section. Boolean operations and variables or constants can be combined to produce more complex expresions using parenthesis, which may be nested to any level.

```
x=1; y=2; z=3
P=x>y; Q=x<y; R=x<z; S=x>z
P,Q,R,S
```

```
(False, True, True, False)
```

```
(P or Q) and (P or S or Q) and (P or R)
```

```
True
```

What we would like to do is to write a general truth expresion for a statement, such as

$$(P \vee Q) \wedge (P \vee S \vee Q) \wedge (P \vee R) \tag{1.1}$$

and then have Python print a truth table. This would require Python to first determine all possible truth values for the tuple (P, Q, R, S) (there are $2^4 = 16$ or them, as we discussed above). Then we would have to substitute these values into the corresponding variables in equation (1.1). Next, we would have to evaluate the truth value of the expression. Finally, we would print out the tuple of input values and final truth value. After some modification for pretty printing, this gives us an algorithm for printing the truth table.

Algorithm for Printing a Truth Table.

> **input:** f: a boolean function of n boolean values
> for each possible combination $b_1, b_2, \ldots, b_n$, $b_i \in \{T,F\}$:
>   print the sequence $b_1, b_2, \ldots, b_n$
>   print $y = f(x_1, x_2, \ldots)$

Defining a truth function for an expression is easy in Python: just define a Python function of the n variables that returns the expression.

```
def f(P,Q,R,S):
    return ((P or Q) and (P or S or Q) and (P or R))
```

Next, we have to call **f** 16 times, one for each combination of truth values. There are two problems here. First, if we want to define a general function **TruthTable(f)** that has only a single parameter **f**, we don't know how many parameters **f** has. So we don't know whether we have to generate 4, or 8, or 16, or 32, etc. combinations. Next, we don't want to have hard-code all those possible cases as multiply-nested loops.

The first problem can be solved using the Python **inspect** library. To import a library, we include the statement:

```
import inspect
```

somewhere near the top of our notebook, and be sure to evaluate it once before we use anything in the library. We want to look at the function **signature(f).parameters** to get the parameters of **f**:

```
inspect.signature(f).parameters
```

```
mappingproxy({'P': <Parameter "P">,
              'Q': <Parameter "Q">,
              'R': <Parameter "R">,
              'S': <Parameter "S">})
```

This gives us far more information than we need. All we are really interested in is the number of parameters, which we can get by counting the number of parameters with the **len** function. The **len** functin works on any sequence data type.

```
len(inspect.signature(f).parameters)
```

```
4
```

For the sake of code readability, we will define a function that will return the number of parameters:

```
def nparams(f):
    return len(inspect.signature(f).parameters)
nparams(f)
```

```
4
```

To get all of the possible combinations we will calculate a cartesian product. A **Cartesian product** of two lists is a list of pairs (x, y) where x is from the first list and y is from the second list. A Cartesian product of n lists $A_1, A_2, \ldots, A_n$ is an exhaustive list of tuples $(a_1, a_2, \ldots, a_n)$ where a_1 taken from the first list, a_2 from A_2, and so forth. The function **product** in the library **itertools** computes the Cartesian product.

```
import itertools
list(itertools.product([0,1],[2,3]))
```

```
[(0, 2), (0, 3), (1, 2), (1, 3)]
```

Mathematically we would write this using the notation

$$[0, 1] \times [2, 3] = [(0, 2), (0, 3), (1, 2), (1, 3)]$$

Since it is somewhat inconvenient to type something like this:

```
list(itertools.product([10,20],[10,20],[10,20]))
```

when we are taking a cartesian product of a set with itself, **itertools** has a parameter **repeat** which allows for this possibility:

```
list(itertools.product([10,20],repeat=3))
```

which means find the Cartesian product of three identical lists,

$$[10, 20] \times [10, 20] \times [10, 20]$$

Ch. 1. Logic and Truth Tables

To compute a truth table of 2 variables, we need to find
$$[\textbf{True},\textbf{False}]\times[\textbf{True},\textbf{False}]$$

For a truth table of 3 variables, we need the Cartesian product
$$[\textbf{True},\textbf{False}]\times[\textbf{True},\textbf{False}]\times[\textbf{True},\textbf{False}]$$

and so on. For a table with **n** variables, this would be

```
itertools.product([True, False],repeat=n)
```

(We did not include the **list** here because we are not tryting to print it out.)

We are almost there. All we need to do is figure out how to pass a sequence of n variables to a function **f**. The problem here is that **f** is expecting the function call as **f(A, B, C, ...)**, and we have the variables returned as tuples:

```
for combo in itertools.product([True, False],\
    repeat=nparams(f)):
    print(combo)
```

```
(True, True, True, True)
(True, True, True, False)
(True, True, False, True)
(True, True, False, False)
(True, False, True, True)
(True, False, True, False)
    ... (additional output omitted) ...
```

We can't just write **f(combo)** because that would be, for example, **f((True, False, True, False))**, where we really want **f(True, False, True, False)**. There is an extra parenthesis in the first case, so we are only passing a single parameter, not all four. The result would be a run-time error. Instead we need to unpack the variables in the list. Unpacking variables is performed using the splat operator in Python: **f(*x)** means unpack the contents of the list **x** and place them right here. The expression **f(*x)** is typicall read as "f splat x." Thus **f(*[3,7,8])** is the same thing as **f(3,7,8)**.

Now we can put together the entire truth table fuction.

```
import itertools, inspect

def nparams(f):
    return len(inspect.signature(f).parameters)

def TruthTable(f):
    n=nparams(f)
    for j in range(n):    # column labels
        print(" {0:6s}".format(chr(65+j)), end="")

    print("| f\n"+6*n*"-"+"+"+"------")   # draw a line

    alltuples = itertools.product([True,False],repeat=n)
    for combination in alltuples:
        for value in combination:
            print (" {0:6s}".format(str(value)), end="")
        result = f(*combination)
        print ("| {0:6s}".format(str(result)))
```

Lets test it out.

```
def f(P,Q,R,S):
    return ((P or Q) and (P or S or Q) and (P or R))
TruthTable(f)
```

A	B	C	D	f
True	True	True	True	True
True	True	True	False	True
True	True	False	True	True
True	True	False	False	True
True	False	True	True	True
True	False	True	False	True
True	False	False	True	True
True	False	False	False	True
False	True	True	True	True
False	True	True	False	True
False	True	False	True	False
False	True	False	False	False
False	False	True	True	False
False	False	True	False	False
False	False	False	True	False
False	False	False	False	False

Quantifiers

Quantifiers are used to specify the scope of a statement or sentence. For example, consider the sentence

"All dogs are blue."

The scope of this statement is *all dogs*. This is an example of **universal quantification**, meaning we a making a statement about everything in a collection of objects. To state this more precisely, we could define two functions:

- **blue(x)** which is **True** when **x** is blue, and **False** otherwise;
- **Dog(x)** that is **True** only when **x** is a dog.

A sentence that depends on a logical **variable** is called a **predicate**, such that when the variable is instantiated, the predicate has a truth value. The expressions **Dog(x)** and **blue(x)** are both predicates. We might then have

$$\text{Dog(Lassie)} = \text{True}$$
$$\text{Dog(HuckelberryHound)} = \text{True}$$
$$\text{Dog(Garfield)} = \text{False}$$

but

$$\text{blue(Lassie)} = \text{False}$$
$$\text{blue(HuckelberryHound)} = \text{True}$$

Suppose define the statement

$$P(x) : \textbf{Dog(x)} \Rightarrow \textbf{blue(x)}$$

The statement $P(x)$ is an example of a predicate, because it depends on a variable x. If we were to instantiate x (give x a value) such as $x =$ Lassie, then $P(\text{Lassie})$ is either **True** or **False**. Until we assigned a value to x, $P(x)$ did not have a truth value.

If we wanted to say that $P(x)$ is true for all values of x, we would write

$$(\forall x)(P(x))$$

---

although it would be more appropriate to write

$$(\forall x \in D)(P(x))$$

Here D is the domain from which we are allowed to choose the values of x. The symbol "$\forall$" is read as "**for all**" and is called a **universal quantifier**.

The expression $(\forall x)(P(x))$ is read as "for all x, $P(x)$."

The expression $(\forall x \in D)(P(x))$ is read as "for all x in D, $P(x)$."

Then we could compose the universally quantified statement: "For all fictional animals, if the animal is a dog, it is blue."

$$(\forall x \in \text{Animals})(\text{Dog}(x) \Rightarrow \text{Blue}(x))$$

Next, consider the statement

"A blue dog is barking."

The scope of this statement is *a single dog*. This is an example of **existential quantification**, meaning we a making a statement about the existence of (at least) one particular item that has a particular property. To state this more precisely, we could define the following function, in addition to **bark(x)** and **Dog(x)**:

• **Barking(x)** that is **True** only when x is barking.

Then if we define the statement
$$Q(x) : \textbf{Dog(x)} \land \textbf{blue(x)} \land \textbf{Barking(x)}$$

we would write
$$(\exists x)(Q(x))$$

which we read as "there exists an x such that $Q(x)$." pecifically in this case, we might read this as "there exists an animal that is a dog and is blue and is barking." The symbol $\exists$ is called the **universal quantifier**.

A universally quantified statement $(\forall x)(P(x))$ says that $P(x)$ is always **True**. It only takes a single counter-example to disprove a universally quantified statement. Thus the existence of a single example of the negation proves the negation:

$$\neg(\forall x)(P(x)) \equiv (\exists x)(\neg P(x))$$

To see this, consider the statement $P(x)$: "all dogs are blue." The negation of this is "It is not true that all dogs are blue." Thus there must be (there exists) at least one dog that is not blue.

Alternatively, consider the statement "there is a blue dog." The negation of this is "it is not true that there is a blue dog." Thus it must be true that all dogs are not blue. In other words, for every dog you come across, that dog is not blue. So we get a similar statement for the negation of existential quantification:

$$\neg(\exists x)(Q(x)) \equiv (\forall x)(\neg Q(x))$$

▶ ▶ ▶ **Example 1.1.** Let $P(x) : x^2 > 0$. Then if x is a real number, the statement $(\forall x)(P(x))$ is **False**, because we can provide a single counter-example ($x = 0$) which is not positive. ◀ ◀ ◀

▶ ▶ ▶ **Example 1.2.** Let $P(x)$ be the statement "There is a perfect square that is a prime number." Then $(\exists x)(P(x))$ is **False**, since for any x that is a perfect square, there is a y such that $x = y \times y$, hence y is a factor of x. ◀ ◀ ◀

We can combine quantifiers from left to right. To specify a general formula for adding fractions, for example, we want to make it universal to all integers. In the following example, for every a, b, c, d, there exists an x and y such that we can add the two fractions together. (In fact, we know that $y = bd$ and $x = ad + bc$.)

▶ ▶ ▶ **Example 1.3.** To describe the addition of fractions over the positive integers, we could write

$$(\forall a)(\forall b)(\forall c)(\forall d)(\exists x)(\exists y)\left(\frac{a}{b} + \frac{c}{d} = \frac{x}{y}\right)$$

◀ ◀ ◀

Exercises

1. Write a truth table to show that $P \Leftrightarrow Q$ and $(P \wedge Q) \vee (\neg P \wedge \neg Q)$ have the same truth values.

2. Write a truth table to show that $P \Leftrightarrow Q$ and $(\neg P \vee Q) \wedge (\neg Q \vee P)$ have the same truth values.

3. Write a truth table to show that $P \wedge (Q \vee R)$ and $(P \wedge Q) \vee (P \wedge R)$ have the same truth value.

4. Write logical expressions and truth tables for the **NAND**, **NOR**, **XNOR**, and **XOR** operations.

5. Of the 16 possible operations on two variables, the text discusses four and exercise 4 discusses four more. Two more are constant functions. This leaves the six remaining unnamed operations. The text claims that these can all be expressed in term so fthe basic operations. Find logical expressions for these six operations. Start by identifying all sixteen operations with a truth table.

6. Modify **TruthTable(f)** to print one letter T or F instead of the entire string **True** or **False**.

7. Python does not have a built in implementation for $A \Rightarrow B$. Implement a function **ifthen(A, B)** that returns the value of $A \Rightarrow B$. Then use **TruthTable** to print

the truth tables of the following:

  a) $(P \Rightarrow Q) \wedge (Q \Rightarrow P)$
  b) $(P \wedge Q) \Rightarrow (R \vee (Q \wedge S))$

8. Python does not have a built in implementation for $A \Leftrightarrow B$. Implement a function **iff(A, B)** that returns the value of $A \Leftrightarrow B$.

9. Instead of using the splat operater in your implementation of **TruthTable**, see if you do it with strings and the **eval** function, but without changing the user interface or code generality in any way. You should only have to replace the **f(*x)** line in your code. Hint: convert the tuple to a string, concatenate the string function name **f.__name__** and then use **eval**. Are there any dangers or pitfalls to this method versus merely unpacking the tuple?

10. The **converse** of $P \Rightarrow Q$ is defined as $Q \Rightarrow P$. Does an implication have the same truth table as its converse?

11. The **contrapositive** of $P \Rightarrow Q$ is defined as $\neg Q \Rightarrow \neg P$. Does an implication have the same truth table as its contrapositive?

12. The **inverse** of $P \Rightarrow Q$ is defined as $\neg P \Rightarrow \neg Q$. Does an implication have the same truth table as its inverse? Can you think of another name for the inverse?

       Ch. 1. Logic and Truth Tables

2. Equivalence

A statement is called a **tautology** if it is always **True**. An example is $P \vee \neg P$. Regardless of the truth value of P, either P will be **True**, or P will be **False**, in which case $\neg P$ will be **True**. The distinguishing property of a tautology is that the final column of its truth table is filled entirely with T:

P	$\neg P$	$P \vee \neg P$
T	F	T
F	T	T

The opposite of a tautology is a **contradiction**. The truth value of a contradiction is always **False**. An example is $P \wedge \neg P$. Since a sentence cannot be both **True** and **False** at the sametime, this is a contradiction. The distinguishing property of a contradiction is that the final column of its truth table is filled entirely with F:

P	$\neg P$	$P \wedge \neg P$
T	F	F
F	T	F

Two statements are said to be **equivalent** if they have the same truth table. We denote equivalence with the $\equiv$ symbol, as in

$$(P \Rightarrow Q) \equiv (\neg P \vee Q) \tag{2.1}$$

Students (and professionals) frequently confuse the use of equivalence and **iff**, denoted by the $\Leftrightarrow$ symbol. The expression

$$(P \Rightarrow Q) \Leftrightarrow (\neq P \vee Q) \tag{2.2}$$

has a different meaning than eq. (2.1). Equation 2.2 has a truth value for each assignment of truth values to P and Q; equation 2.1 does not. Equation 2.1 means that both sentences have the same semantic meaning. The semantic meaning of a sentence is its truth table. Thus we write eq. 2.1 to say that eq. 2.2 is a tautology, that is, it has a truth value of **True**, regardless of the the truth assignments of P and Q.

In general we will say that P and Q are equivalent (and write $P \equiv Q$) if $P \Leftrightarrow Q$ is a tautology. An example is De Morgan's Laws.

Table 2.1. De Morgan's Laws.
$\neg(p \wedge q) \equiv \neg p \vee \neg q$ $\neg(p \vee q) \equiv \neg p \wedge \neg q$

At this point in our study, the only method we have to prove equivalence is via a truth table. To prove De Morgan's Laws we will build a truth table. The truth table for the left hand proposition, $\neg(p \wedge q)$, is in the first 4 columns of the following table. The truth table for the right hand proposition of of De Morgan's first law, $\neg p \vee \neg q$, is in columns 1, 2, and 5 through 7.

(1)	(2)	(3)	(4)	(5)	(6)	(7)
p	q	$p \wedge q$	$\neg(p \wedge q)$	$\neg p$	$\neg q$	$\neg p \vee \neg q$
T	T	T	F	F	F	F
T	F	F	T	F	T	T
F	T	F	T	T	F	T
F	F	F	T	T	T	T

The truth values of the two propositions are giving by the final columns. For the left hand side, these are in column 4, and are given by the ordered {F, T, T, T}. For the right hand side, the output is in column 7, and are also {F, T, T, T}. For two propositions to be equivalent, they must have the same output for the same input. In a truth table, that means they must have the same output in the same order. Since the two ordered sets are equal, the propositions are equivalent.

The other logical equivalences shown in the table can also be proven by truth table. Several of these equivalences are similar to the algebraic properties of the real numbers. For example:

- In the real numbers, we define an **identity** for multplication (addition) as a number 1 (0) such that $1 \cdot x = x$ ($0 + x = x$). Thecorresponding identity for for **and** (**or**) is F (T).
- The double negative under addition $-(-x) = x$ is analgous to double negation. For example, $-(-3) = 3$.

- Associative properites of addition and multiplication are analogous to the associative properties of **and** and **or**.
- We may distribute multiplication over addition in the real numbers, e.g, $a(b + c) = ab + ac$, although we may not distribute addition over multiplicaiton $(a + bc \neq (a + b)(a + c)$, in general). We can distribute $\wedge$ over $\vee$ and vice-versa.

Table 2.2. Logical Equivalences.

Identities	**Associative Laws**
$p \wedge T \equiv p$	$(p \vee q) \vee r \equiv p \vee (q \vee r)$
$p \vee F \equiv p$	$(p \wedge q) \wedge r \equiv p \wedge (q \wedge r)$
Domination Laws	**Distributive Laws**
$p \vee T \equiv T$	$p \vee (p \wedge q) \equiv (p \vee q) \wedge (p \vee q)$
$p \wedge F \equiv F$	$p \wedge (p \vee q) \equiv (p \wedge q) \vee (p \wedge q)$
Idempotent Laws	**Absorption Laws**
$p \vee p \equiv p$	$p \vee (p \wedge q) \equiv p$
$p \wedge p \equiv p$	$p \wedge (p \vee q) \equiv p$
Double Negation	
$\neg(\neg p) \equiv p$	

We can prove additional equivalences using the rules in table 2.1.

▶ ▶ ▶ **Example 2.1.** Prove that $\neg(p \Rightarrow q) \equiv (p \wedge \neg q)$

Proof. Starting with the left hand side of the expression,

$$\neg(p \Rightarrow q) \equiv \neg(\neg p \vee q)) \qquad \text{By definition on page 5}$$
$$\equiv \neg(\neg p) \wedge \neg q \qquad \text{By De Morgans Law}$$
$$\equiv p \wedge \neg q \qquad \text{By the Double Negation Law} \quad \square$$

□

◀ ◀ ◀

▶ ▶ ▶ **Example 2.2.** Prove that $\neg(p \vee (\neg p \wedge \neg q)) \equiv (\neg p \wedge q)$

Proof. Starting with the left hand side of the expression,

$$\neg(p \vee (\neg p \wedge \neg q))$$
$$\equiv \neg p \wedge \neg(\neg p \wedge \neg q) \qquad \text{De Morgan's Law}$$
$$\equiv \neg p \wedge (\neg\neg p \vee \neg\neg q) \qquad \text{De Morgan's Law}$$

$$\equiv \neg p \wedge (p \vee q) \qquad \text{Double Negation}$$
$$\equiv (\neg p \wedge p) \vee (\neg p \wedge q) \qquad \text{Distributive Law}$$
$$\equiv F \vee (\neg p \wedge q) \qquad P \wedge \neg P \text{ is a}$$

contradiction; see p. 17

$$\equiv \neg p \wedge q \qquad F \text{ is an identity under } \vee$$

□

◄ ◄ ◄

Equivalences in Python

We can use our function **TruthTable** to determine equivalences. All we really want to do is compare the right-hand column of two different tables. So we modify the truth table function to only return a list of the results, rather than actually print the table. Then we compare the two lists.

```
import itertools, inspect
def TruthTableResult(f):
    result=[]
    for combination in itertools.product([True,False],\
      repeat=len(inspect.signature(f).parameters) ):
        result.append(f(*combination))
    return(result)

def equiv(f, g):
        return(TruthTableResult(f)==TruthTableResult(g))
```

Exercises

1. The exclusive or function, $A \oplus B$, can be determined by the following truth table:

A	B	$A \oplus B$
T	T	F
T	F	T
F	T	T
F	F	F

   Show that $A \oplus B \equiv (A \vee B) \wedge \neg(A \wedge B)$

2. Prove De Morgan's second law using a truth table.

3. Use a truth table (either by hand or with a computer program) to prove the commutative laws for $\wedge$ and $\vee$.

4. Use a truth table (either by hand or with a computer program) to prove the associative laws for $\wedge$ and $\vee$.

5. Use a truth table (either by hand or with a computer program) to prove the distributive laws.

6. Use a truth table (either by hand or with a computer program) to prove the absorption laws.

7. Verify all of the logical equivalences in the table on page 19 using the Python function **equiv** defined in the text.

8. A statement is said to be **satisfiabile** if there is some association of possible truth values for each of the variables such that the expression becomes **True**. For example, $p \vee q$ is satisfiable for $(p, q) =$(T,T), (T,F), or (F,T). However, $p \wedge \neg p$ is not satisfiable, because there is not any possible assignment of values that will ever make it **True**. Write a Python function that will determine if a statement is satisfiable, and if so, return a list of assignments of T and F values that make the statement **True**.

9. Either by using the function written in exercise 8 or by writing truth tables by hand, determine if each of the following is satisfiable, and if so, return a list of all the possible solutions.

   a) $(p \vee q \vee r) \wedge (p \wedge q) \vee (p \vee q)$
   b) $(p \wedge q) \vee (p \wedge r) \vee (q \wedge r)$
   c) $(p \vee q \vee r) \wedge (p \vee q \vee s) \wedge (q \vee r \vee s) \wedge (p \vee r \vee s)$

3. Argument and Proof

An **argument** is a sequence of statements. The final statement is called the **conclusion**; the remaining statements are called **premises**. We say that an argument is valid if, regardless of the statements, if all of the variables are **True** then the conclusion is **True**.

We can test that an argument is valid by constructing its truth table, as follows:

1. Identify all the premises

2. Construct a truth table with columns for all the premises and the conclusion

3. If in any row, (a) all the premises are **True** and (b) the conclusion is **False** then the argument is invalid.

4. If in every row in which all the premises are **True** the conclusion is also **True**, then the argument is valid.

The mathematical proofs that we are interested in will be composed of sequences of arguments. A conceptual description of an argument is called an **argument form**. The most commonly used argument form is called the syllogism. A **syllogism** is an argument with two premises and a conclusion. The first premise is referred to as the **major premise**, and the second premise is called the **minor premise**. We sometimes precede the statement of the conclusion with the symbol $\therefore$ (meaning therefore), as in: $\therefore Q$, meaning "therefore Q is **True**." Common syllogisms and other argument forms include

- *modus ponens* is equivalent to the tautology $(P \wedge (P \Rightarrow Q)) \Rightarrow Q$. We summarize *modus ponens* in detail here.

  1. $P \Rightarrow Q$, stating the major premise. The major premise of *modus ponens* is always some sort of if-then statement that we can simlify to the form $P \Rightarrow Q$, where P and Q are statements.
  2. P, stating the minor premise, which in this case is our claim that P is true. The minor premise of *modus ponens* is always

the sufficiency (left hand side) of the implication $P \Rightarrow Q$ that is stated in step 1. Usually this is a restatement of some observation, fact, or conculusion that has been made in a long sequence of these argument steps.

3. $\therefore Q$ (concluding that Q is true).

► ► ► **Example 3.1.** Demonstrate that the integer 7 is rational.

1. $(7 = 7/1) \Rightarrow (7 \in \mathbb{Q})$ by the definition of rational numbers.
2. $(7 = 7/1)$ by the definition of unity.
3. $\therefore 7 \in \mathbb{Q}$ by *modus ponens*.

◄ ◄ ◄

- *modus tollens*, is equivalent to $(\neg Q \wedge (P \Rightarrow Q)) \Rightarrow \neg P)$, and can be summarized in the following 3-step argument.

1. $P \Rightarrow Q$ (Step 1 is always some $\Rightarrow$.)
2. $\neg Q$ (Step 2 is always the right hand argument of the $\Rightarrow$.)
3. $\therefore \neg P$

► ► ► **Example 3.2.** Demonstrate that 15 is odd:

1. (15 is even) $\Rightarrow$ (15 is divisible by 2 without remainder) by the definition of an even number.
2. $15/2=7$ with a remainder of 1 so $\neg$(15 is divisible by 2 without remainder), i.e., the right hand argument of the $\Rightarrow$ operator is false.
3. Therefore $\neg$(15 is even), by *modus tonens*.

Since the negation of (15 is even) is (15 is odd), this demonstrates that 15 is odd. ◄ ◄ ◄

- **disjunctive syllogism**, also called **elimination**, is equivalent to $((P \vee q) \wedge \neg P) \Rightarrow Q$. We summarize it in the following 3-step summary.

1. $P \vee Q$
2. $\neg P$
3. $\therefore Q$

► ► ► **Example 3.3.**

1. 16 is either even or it is odd.
2. 16 is not odd.

3. Therefore 16 is even by a disjunctive syllogism or the processe of elimination.

◄ ◄ ◄

- A **Hypothetical syllogism**, also called the **transitivity of the if/then**, is equivalent to $((P \Rightarrow Q) \land (Q \Rightarrow R)) \Rightarrow (P \Rightarrow R)$. A hypothetical syllogistm starts with two if/then statements, where the "then" of the first is the same as the "if" of the second. This is where transitivity kicks in, essentially cancelling out the middle argument. It can be summarized as any argument of the following format:

  1. $P \Rightarrow Q$
  2. $Q \Rightarrow R$
  3. $\therefore\ P \Rightarrow R$

Occasionally this will be written as $P \Rightarrow Q \Rightarrow R$, thus $P \Rightarrow R$.

▶ ▶ ▶ **Example 3.4.**

1. If T is an equilateral triangle then it is a regular polygon.
2. If P is a regular polygon then it is convex.
3. By a hypothetical syllogism, If T is an equilateral triangle, then it is convex.

◄ ◄ ◄

- **Resolution** is equivalent to $((P \lor Q) \land (\neg P \lor R)) \Rightarrow (Q \lor R)$. It is described by the following three steps:

  1. $P \lor Q$
  2. $\neg P \lor R$
  3. $\therefore\ Q \lor R$

- **Generalization**, equivalent to $P \Rightarrow (P \lor Q)$

  1. P
  2. $\therefore\ P \lor Q$

- **Simplification** or **specialization**, equivalent to $(P \land Q) \Rightarrow P$.

  1. $P \land Q$

2. $\therefore P$

All of these argument forms can also be understood in terms of the analogy with sets (see the argument method of proofs in chapter 4). It sometimes helps students to draw Venn diagrams to understand this. However, this could lead to a circular argument and should not be used to actually justify the argument forms listed here, becuase it it is the logical connectives ($\vee$ and $\wedge$) that are used to define set relationships (operators $\cup$, $\cap$, $\subseteq$) in the first place.

▶ ▶ ▶ **Example 3.5.** Suppose that we know there are 7 pigeon holes in the tree in the back yard, and we have seen 8 pigeons outside. If we define

$P =$ "There are more pigeons than pigeon holes"

$Q =$ "At least two pigeons must share a pigeon hole"

Then we can argue:

$P \Rightarrow Q$ The Pigeonhole Principle

P Since there are 7 holes and 8 Pigeons

$\therefore Q$ Modus Ponens

And therefore at least two pigeons share the same hole.   ◀ ◀ ◀

When making an argument we must be careful to avoid making an mistake in the sequence of steps that lead to the conclusion. methods A **fallacy** is an error in reasoning that leads to an invalid argument. Common fallacies include

1. Ambiguous premises

2. Circular reasoning (assuming what is to be proven)

3. Jumping to a conclusion (with an adequate reason)

4. Misapplication of the converse and the inverse

Sometimes we will find it helpful to number the statements in an argument or proof (you may recall two-colum proofs from an elementary geometry or pre-calculus class, for example, where the steps were numbered). This is not strictly necesary, and we will not do it most of the time (especially in mathematical proofs). However, numbering steps helps to delineate the chain of reasoning, e.g., step 1 to step 2 to step 3, etc.

▶ ▶ ▶ **Example 3.6.** (An example of converse error.)

1. If Joe is a cheater, then Joe sits in the back row.
2. Joe is sitting in the back row.
3. ∴ Joe is a cheater.

◄ ◄ ◄

▶ ▶ ▶ **Example 3.7.** (An example of inverse error.)

1. If interest rates go up, stock prices go down.
2. Interest rates are not going up.
3. ∴ stock prices will not go down.

◄ ◄ ◄

It is also possible to make a perfectly valid argument, but it will lead to an incorrect conclusion if there are false premises.

▶ ▶ ▶ **Example 3.8.** (A Valid Arguments with False Premises)

1. If John Lennon was a rock star then John Lennon had green hair.
2. John Lennon was a rock start
3. Therefore John Lennon had green hair.

◄ ◄ ◄

Alternatively, we can reach a valid conclusion with a true premise even though we use an invalid argument.

▶ ▶ ▶ **Example 3.9.** The conclusion of the following argument is true, but it is an invalid argument. This one makes improper use of the converse to achieve a correct result.

1. If New York is a big city, then it has tall buildings
2. New York has tall buildings.
3. Therefore, New York is a big city.

◄ ◄ ◄

An argument is **sound** if and only if (a) it is valid and (b) all of its premises are true. Otherwise the argument is called an **unsound argument**.

In mathematics we would like to prove statements are true using sound, valid arguments. We will discuss several different methods of proof throughout this text; all of these techniques draw on the tools and techniques of logic and inference. The principle methods we will discuss are:

- **Direct proof** is the most basic form proof. It uses a straigtforward chain of inference to derive one result from another. The first step is the list of assumptions or "givens." Then each succeding step is derived from the previous steps by the rules of inference. The final step is the conclusion. We will apply use direct proof to develop some results from elementary number theory in chapter 5.

- Proof by **contraposition** is based on the following observation: a proof that $\neq Q \Rightarrow \neq P$ is **True** is just as good as a proof that $P \Rightarrow Q$ is **True**. This is because

$$(P \Rightarrow Q) \equiv (\neg Q \Rightarrow \neg P)$$

We will discuss proof by contraposition in more detail in chapter 8.

- Proof by **contradiction** is based upon the following **contradiction rule**: assume that $\neg P =$ **True**. Then by a valid chain of inference, show that this leads either to a nonsense statement, such as $1 = 0$, or to a logical contradiction, such as $(Q =$**True**$) \wedge (Q =$**False**$)$. Then we conclude that $P =$ **True**. We will discuss proof by contradiction in more detail in chapter 9.

- Proof by **cases**. Sometimes the way we need to look at how something will vary with a parameter of the problem. For example, if we want o prove a property $P(k)$ of the integers, the analysis may be very different if k is even or if k is odd. So we divide the proof up into multiple parts, called cases, and prove the statement separately for each case. Here (in this example of even vs. odd) we might cite two cases: then we first prove $P(k)$ where k is even; and then prove $P(k)$ where k is odd. There is no restriction on the number of cases or the way we break things down. In some situations there could be millions of possibly different cases (e.g., the four color map theorem) that need to be considered and the proof would then require computer assistance.

- Proof by **counter-example**. A universally quantified statement can be disproven by a single counter-example. Similarly, an existentially quantified statement can also be proven by a single example. This will be discussed in chapter 7.

- Proof by **induction** proves that a statement $P(k)$ is **True** for all integers $k > a$ for some starting integer a. The basic idea is this: (a)

First we prove that $P(a)$ is **True**. Then we assume that $P(n)$ is **True** for $n > a$ and use direct proof (or any other method) to demonstrate that $P(n) \Rightarrow P(n+1)$. Proof by induction is discussed in more detail in chapter 10.

Pointers for writing proofs

Existential proofs are for theorems of the form $(\exists x)(P(x))$ where $P(x)$ is some sentence. Such proofs may be constructive, in which case the actual value of some number a for which $P(a)$ is true, is produced. Otherwise, the proof is not constructive.

In a **constructive existential proof**, usually one of the following two approaches is taken:

1. Provide some value of a for which $P(a)$ is true (and prove $P(a)$)

2. Provide a sequence of instructions that leads one to obtain the at least one a (or a set all some a, or all possible a) for which $P(a)$ is true.

If the existential proof is **not constructive**, then typical approaches are

1. Show by a sequence of logical arguments that some x must exist that makes $P(x)$ true. This sequence may follow form previously stated theorems and theorems, and must follow a valid chain of logic.

2. Show that the assumption that no such x exists will lead to logical contradiction.

A **universal statement** has the form $(\forall x)(P(x))$. To prove a a universal statement we generally use a **method of generalization from the particular to the general**. This means that we pick a value of x at random, but not specific, from the domain, denoted by some variable, say u.i This variable is unrestricted in any other way. Then we prove that $P(u)$. Since there are no restrictions on u, the arguments must be valid for all x in the domain.

To make the proof completely clear and error free, you should always do the following:

- Write down what needs to be proven.

- Clearly mark the beginning of the proof.

- Don't pull new variables out of the air. Everytime you use a new variable, define it. Don't assume that readers know that $P(x)$ is the conjecture you are proving. If that is what mean, say "Let P(x) be the following conjecture: ..." and so forth.

- Write each line of your proof in complete sentences. Every statement has a noun and verb. (Symbols like an equal sign are considered verbs.)

- Justify every line of your proof. It helps to number your steps and then refer back to earlier steps by number or refer to therems, definitions, and axioms by number or name.

- Don't try to save time by saving space. Especially in English, the small words like a, the, if, then, etc., all have a very specific meaning and using them (or not using them) correctly can change the meaning of your proof significantly.

- Make a clear statment when your proof is completed. You may choose to write "QED", or □, or ■, or "this is what were trying to prove." If you are using LaTeX, you may want to use the built in command \qed (for □).

- Some forms of proof require you to specifically label other parts of the proof (such in proof by induction).

Exercises

Convert each of the following arguments into formal statements, e.g., define sentences existentially and/or universally quantified statements. Then determine which rules of logic have been applied and explain whether or not they have been applied correctly.

1. If you do the homework you will pass the final. Somebody did not pass the final. Therefore somebody did not not do the homework.

2. If you do the homework you will pass the final. Curly did not do the homework. Therefore Curly will not pass the final.

3. If you don't do the homework, you won't pass the final. Moe did the homework. Therefore Moe passed the final.

4. If you don't do the homework, you won't pass the final. Curly did not do the homework. Therefore Curly did not pass the final.

5. If you do the homework you will pass the final. If you pass the final you will pass the course. Larry did the homework. Therefore Larry will pass the course.

6. Curly, Moe and Larry are stooges. Curly did his homework. Therefore a stooge did his homework.

7. Curly and Moe are stooges. Therefore Curly is a stooge.

8. All numbers that are divisible by two are even. 17 is not divisible by two. Therefore 17 is not even.

9. If $b^2 > 4ac$ then there are two real roots of $ax^2 + bx + c = 0$ that are given by $(-b \pm \sqrt{b^2 - 4ac})/(2a)$. Therefore $x^2 + 5x + 1 = 0$ has two real roots.

10. If a is any real number then $x^2 + a^2 = 0$ does not have any real solution. Therefore there is no real solution to $x^2 + 4 = 0$.

4. Sets

Definition 4.1. Set

A **set** is an enumerable (listable) collection of distinct objects or items. The items or objects in a set are called the set's **members** or **elements**.

The most comming way of representing a set mathematically is by enumerating (listing) the items in the set, and enclosing the items with curly brackets. This is sometimes called **set roster notation**. For example, the set S that contains the integers 1, 2, and 3 may be written as

$$S = \{1, 2, 3\}$$

We can denote an enumerable pattern using the **ellipsis notation** $(\ldots)$, but only where the pattern is clear from the set description. The set T of all integers between 1 and 100 may be expressed in manner as

$$T = \{1, 2, 3, \ldots, 100\}$$

A set only depends on its elements, and not on how the elements are arranged. This is formalized as the **Axiom of Extension**. Consequently, we might think of a set as being analogous to bag of distinguishible items, and not like an array or list of items in a typical progamming languages, which are more akin to the mathematical concept of a vector.

Definition 4.2. Axiom of Extension

The properties of a set depend only on its elements and not the order or repetition of its elements.

▶ ▶ ▶ **Example 4.1.** We may think of a set as a bag of items that we bring home from the grocery store.

Suppose it contains a can of peas, a loaf of bread, a carton of eggs, and two cans of chicken soup.
{ Peas, Bread, Eggs, Soup, Other Soup }

The items are enumerable and the order does not matter. We have the same groceries regardless of how we remove the groceries from the bag. The items are also distinct, as there must be a way to distinguish between the two cans of chicken soup, such as serial numbers or other markings on the cans. (Or we can eat one can of soup and still have one left, clearly making them distinguishable.)
◀ ◀ ◀

When we want to specify that some item is a member of a set, we use the $\in$ notation ($y \in P$, meaning y is in the set P). We draw to line through the $\in$ to indicate that an item is not in a set (e.g., $x \notin Q$, x is not in Q). Returning to our sets S and T defined above, we have the following:

$$2 \in S$$
$$2 \in T$$
$$27 \notin S$$
$$27 \in T$$

Since sets are not ordered, the set $S = \{1, 2, 3\}$ may also be written as

$$S = \{2, 1, 3\}, \text{ or } S = \{3, 1, 2\}, \text{ or } S = \{1, 3, 2\}, \text{ etc.}$$

Alternatively, we may say that

$$A = \{2, 1, 3\}, \quad B = \{3, 1, 2\}, \quad C = \{1, 3, 2\},$$

where A, B, C, and S are all **equal**. We would write, for example, $A = B$, or

$$\{2, 1, 3\} = \{3, 2, 1\}$$

Formally, we say two sets are equal if every element of each set is in the other set.

Definition 4.3. Set Equality.

We say the sets A and B are **equal**, and write $A = B$, if

$$(\forall x)((x \in A) \iff (x \in B))$$

Furthermore, we say that A and B are **not equal**, and write that $A \neq B$, if either $(\exists x \in B)(x \notin A)$ or $(\exists x \in A)(x \notin B)$.

Python allows us to define sets using set roster notation, and it enforces the Axiom of Extension.

```
S={2,3,4}
T={4,2,3}
print(S==T)
```

```
True
```

Python also does not distinguish between indistinguishible items iff they are placed into a set:

```
TT={2,2,4,4,3};
print(TT)
```

```
{2,3,4}
```

```
{1,2,3,4}=={4,3,1,1,2,4,3}
```

```
True
```

Standard Sets

Standard symbols reserved for some special mathematical sets. These include:

- $\mathbb{Z}$ = The set of all **integers**.

- $\mathbb{Z}^+$ = The set of all **positive integers**.

- $\mathbb{N}$ = The set of all **natural numbers** (positive integers or zero).

- $\mathbb{Q}$ = The set of all **rational** numbers. A number x is said to be rational if there exist two integers a, b, with $b \neq 0$, such that $= x/b$. If no such integers exist, then we say that x is **irrational**. An example of an irrational number is $\sqrt{7}$.

- $\mathbb{R}$ = The set of all **Real** numbers. A number is real if it is either rational or irrational.

- $\mathbb{R}^+$ = The set of all positive real numbers.

- $\mathbb{C}$ = the set of all **complex numbers**, sometimes referred to as the **complex plane**.

Set Builder Notation

We will sometimes define sets using **set builder notation**. Set builder notation expresses a set using a rule, as in "S is the set of all x that have the property $P(x)$," and written as

$$\{x|P(x)\}$$

For example the set S of all even integers greater than 17 may be written as

$$S = \{x|(x \in \mathbb{Z}) \text{ and } (x \text{ is even}) \text{ and } (x > 17)\}$$

Often when x is chosen from one of the standard mathematical sets, we wr rite that on the left hand side of the vertical bar:

$$S = \{x \in \mathbb{Z}|(x \text{ is even}) \text{ and } (x > 17)\}$$

Similarly, if we are refining one set to form another, we put the orignal set on the left. If we define $\mathbb{E}$ as the set of even integers, then we might also choose to write

$$S = \{x \in \mathbb{E}|x > 17\}$$

▶ ▶ ▶ **Example 4.2.** Write the set $A = \{-3, -2, -1, 0, 1, 2, 3, 4, 5\}$ using set builder notation.

Since this set contains all the integers between -3 and 5, one way to do this is
$A = \{x \in \mathbb{Z}| -3 \leqslant x \leqslant 5\}$. ◀ ◀ ◀

Python's **set comprehension** provides an implementation of set builder notatoin. Set comprehension is analogous to the more commonly used list comprehension feature of python. For example to define the set of all even integers between less than 25 that are divisible by 5, using set builder notation we could say

$$S = \{x \in \mathbb{Z}^+|(x < 25) \wedge (x \bmod 2 = 0) \wedge (x \bmod 5 = 0)\}$$

where the mod operator is the modulus, or remainder, after integer division. In python, the integer remainder is given by the percent sign.

Here we define two predicates: `P(j)` and `Q(j)`. The first one returns **True** if `j` is even, and **False** otherwise. The second one (**P**) returns **True** if `j` is divisible by 5, and **False** otherwise. The set **R25** is an enumeration of the integers $\{0, 1, \ldots, 24\}$. Then **S** is the set of all items in **R25** that satisfy both `P(j)` and `Q(j)`, namely, they are divisible both by 2 and 5.

```
def P(j):          # Return True if j is even
    return j%2==0
def Q(j):          # Return True if j is multiple of 5
    return j%5==0
R25={j for j in range(25)}
S={j for j in R25 if (P(j) and Q(j))}
print(S)
```

{0, 10, 20}

We could also have written the entire set comprehension as a single line,

```
{j for j in range(25) if j%2==0 and j%5==0}
```

{0, 10, 20}

Cardinality

One measure of a set is the count of the number of elements in a set. We call this count its **cardinality**. A finite set has a finite cardinality. For example, the cardinality of $\{\text{Curly}, \text{Moe}, \text{Larry}\}$ is 3. In python, we calculate the cardinality of a finite set with the **len** function, just as we do for a finite list.

If we can place a set in one-to-one correspondence with the positive integers, then we say that the set is **countable, enumerable,** or **countably infinite**. Examples of countable sets are $\mathbb{N}$, $\mathbb{Q}$, and $\mathbb{Z}$. Sets that are larger than the integers, such as the real numbers, are called uncountable.

Proofs About Sets

We will often find in necessary to prove properties of sets. In general, there are two different methods for doing this: **element argments** and **identity argments**. As implied by their names, element arguments are based on examining the elements of sets, and identity elements are based on applying sequences or combinations of identities. Anything that can be proven with an element argument can also be proven with an identity argument and vice-versa.

Definition 4.4. Subset

A collection of objects that is contained in another collection is said to be a **subset** of the larger set. Formally, we say that A is a subset of B if $(\forall x \in A)(x \in B)$ and we write $A \subseteq B$:

$$A \subseteq B \equiv ((\forall x \in A)(x \in B))$$

If $A \subseteq B$ and $A \neq B$, then A is a **proper subset** of B and we write:

$$A \subset B \equiv ((A \subseteq B) \wedge (A \neq B))$$

We observe that according to definition 4, every set includes both itself and the empty set as subsets. If $A \subset B$, then $(\exists x \in B)(x \notin A)$, but not vice-versa. Thus the empty set is a proper subset of every non-empty set.

For example, **element argument** can be used to prove that one $A \subseteq B$. To do this we

- Let $x \in A$ be an element of A. We cannot place any restrictions on which element of A we choose; any element is allowed to be chosen arbitrarily or at random.

- Prove that $x \in B$.

- Since we can be prove that any randomly selected element of A is an element of B (without restriction) then we conclude that $(\forall x)((x \in A) \Rightarrow (x \in B))$. This proves that $A \subseteq B$.

► ► ► **Example 4.3.** Prove that $A \subseteq B$, where

$$A = \{m \in \mathbb{Z} | m = 6r + 12 \text{ for some } r \in \mathbb{Z}\}$$
$$B = \{n \in \mathbb{Z} | n = 3s \text{ for some } s \in \mathbb{Z}\}$$

Proof. We will use an element argument.

1. Let $x \in A$. Then by the definition of A, $\exists r \in \mathbb{Z}$ such that

$$x = 6r + 12 = 3(2r + 6)$$

2. Let $s = 2r + 6 \in \mathbb{Z}$ (closure of $\mathbb{Z}$).
3. Then $x = 3s$ (substitution) where $s \in \mathbb{Z}$.
4. This means that $x \in B$ (definitio of B).
5. Since there was no restriction on the choice of x, except that it was a randomly chosen element of B, we conclude that $(\forall x \in A)(x \in B)$.

The last step tells us that $A \subseteq B$. □

Earlier we said that two sets were equal if every element of each set is an element of the other. The proof of this is little more than a formalization of such a statement.

Theorem 4.1.

Let A and B be sets. Then $A = B$ if and only if $A \subseteq B$ and $B \subseteq A$.

Proof. First prove $(A = B) \Rightarrow (A \subseteq B \land B \subseteq A)$.

1. Suppose $A = B$.
2. $(\forall x)((x \in A) \Rightarrow (x \in B))$ (definition of set equality, def. 3).
3. Thus $A \subseteq B$ (step 2 and def. 4).
4. $(\forall x)((x \in B) \Rightarrow (x \in A))$ definition of set equality, def. 3).
5. Thus $B \subseteq A$ (step 4 and def. 4).
6. Thus $A = B \Rightarrow (A \subseteq B \land B \subseteq A)$.

Next, prove that $(A \subseteq B \land B \subseteq A) \Rightarrow (A = B)$.

1. Suppose that $A \subseteq B \land B \subseteq B$.

2. Since $A \subseteq B$, then $(\forall x \in A)(x \in B)$ (def. 4).
3. Since $B \subseteq A$, then $(\forall x \in B)(x \in A)$ (def. 4).
4. Thus by steps 2, 3, and def 3, $A = B$.

Therefore $((\forall x \in A)(x \in B)) \land ((\forall x \in B)(x \in A)) \iff (A = B)$

$\square$

▶ ▶ ▶ **Example 4.4.** Prove that $A = B$, where

$$A = \{n \in \mathbb{Z} | n = 2k \text{ for some } k \in \mathbb{Z}\}$$
$$B = \{m \in \mathbb{Z} | m = 2\ell - 2 \text{ for some } \ell \in \mathbb{Z}\}$$

Proof. We need to show (a) $A \subseteq B$ and (b) $B \subseteq A$.

(a) Proof that $A \subseteq B$.

1. Let $x \in A$.
2. Then $\exists k \in \mathbb{Z}$ such that $x = 2k$ (by definition of A).
3. Define $\ell = k + 1$. Since $k \in \mathbb{Z}$ we know $\ell \in \mathbb{Z}$ (axiom 5.1).
4. By substitution $x = 2(\ell - 1) = 2\ell - 2$. Thus $x \in B$ by the definition of B.
5. This argument holds for any randomly selected $x \in A$. Hence $\forall x \in A$ we conclude that $x \in B$.
6. This implies that $A \subseteq B$ (def. 4).

(b). Proof that $B \subseteq A$.

1. Let $x \in B$.
2. By definition of the set B there exists some $\ell \in \mathbb{Z}$ such that $x = 2\ell - 2$.
3. Let $k = \ell - 1$. Then $x = 2\ell - 2 = 2(\ell - 1) = 2k$ by substitution.
4. Since $\ell \in \mathbb{Z}$, we know that $k \in \mathbb{Z}$ (closure).
5. Hence by the definition of A, $x \in A$.
6. This argument holds for any randomly selected element of B, thus it is true for all elements of B. Thus $(\forall x)((x \in B) \Rightarrow (x \in A))$.
7. Therefore $B \subseteq A$.

Since $A \subseteq B$ and $B \subseteq A$, we conclude that $A = B$. $\square$

◀ ◀ ◀

We can form new sets by considering the **intersection** and **union** of other sets. Two sets are said to intersect if they contain some common elements; the set of elements that are held in common is called their intersection.

A useful tool for illustrating the intersection and union is the **Venn Diagram**. Each set is represented by a blob (circle). The interior of the cirle represents the contents of the set. The rest of the universe is represented by the exterior of the circle. If two circles overlap, that means they share some items in common (see figure 4.1).

Figure 4.1.: The intersection of the sets A and B is represented by the shaded area.

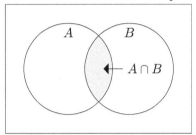

Definition 4.5. Set Intersection

The **Intersection** of two sets A and B is the set $A \cup B$ containing every element that is in both A and B:

$$A \cap B = \{x | (x \in A) \wedge (x \in B)\}$$

If $A_0, A_1, \ldots A_n$ are a (possibly infinitely) enumerable sequence of sets then

$$\bigcap_{i=0}^{n} A_i = \{x | (x \in A_i)(\forall i)\} = \{x | (x \in A_0) \wedge (x \in A_1) \wedge \cdots \wedge (x \in A_n)\}$$

We also write

$$\bigcap_{i=0}^{n} A_i = A_0 \cap A_1 \cap \cdots \cap A_n$$

The union on of two sets (see figure 4.2) contains all items that are in either of the sets. The sets do not necessarily have to intersect and may consist of disjoint blobs in the Venn diagriam after they are filled in.

Definition 4.6. Set Union

The **Union** of two sets A and B is the set $A \cup B$ containing every element in each set:

$$A \cup B = \{x | (x \in A) \vee (x \in B)\}$$

If $A_0, A_1, \ldots A_n$ are a (possibly infinitely) enumerable sequence of sets then

$$\bigcup_{i=0}^{n} A_i = \{x | (x \in A_i) \text{ for a least one } i\} = \{x | (x \in A_0) \vee (x \in A_1) \vee \cdots \vee (x \in A_n)\}$$

We also write

$$\bigcup_{i=0}^{n} A_i = A_0 \cup A_1 \cup \cdots \cup A_n$$

Figure 4.2.: The union of the sets A and B is represented by the shaded area.

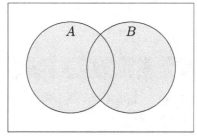

The **complement** of a set A is the set of all items in the domain that are not in A.

Definition 4.7. Set Complement

The complement of the set A consists of all elements in the domain that are not in A and is denoted by $\overline{A}$,

$$\overline{A} = \{x | x \notin A\}$$

▶ ▶ ▶ **Example 4.5.** Consider the "universe" consisting of all the cars at Sam's Used Car Lot (figure 4.3).

Let $R = \{$All red cars for sale at Sam's$\}$.

Then $\overline{R} = \{$All cars for sale at Sam's that are not red$\}$ ◀ ◀ ◀

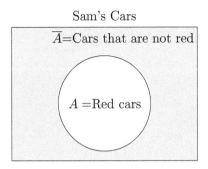

Sam's Cars

▶ ▶ ▶ **Example 4.6.** Let S be the set of all negative integers. Then the complement of S is the non-negative integers. ◀ ◀ ◀

Set complement is closely related to **set difference**. Let's think of $\overline{A}$ as what is left when we "subtract" or remove all the elments in A from the Universe, where by "Universe" we mean the domain over which the elements apply (e.g., Sam's Used Car lot, or all integers). Then we might want to write $\overline{A}$ as

$$\overline{A} = \text{Universe} - A$$

Similarly, if B is *any* set, we can consider what happens if we remove all the elments in A that happen to also be in B; all this set C.

$$C = B - A = \{x | (x \in B) \wedge (x \notin A)\}$$

This is called the **relative complement** of A in B, or the **set difference**.

Definition 4.8. Relative Complement

The **relative complement** of A in B is the part of $\overline{A}$ that is in B and is denoted by $B - A$

$$B - A = B \cap \overline{A} = \{x | (x \in B) \wedge (x \notin A)\}$$

Some textbooks denote the relative complement as $B \setminus A$ rather than $B - A$, but the minus sign is preferable because it emphasizes the "take-away" nature of the operation, and the down-diagonal is easily confused with

---

Figure 4.4.: The relative complement $B - A$ is shaded.

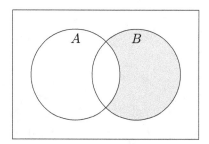

the backslash character used to initiate an escape code in many computer languages.

▶ ▶ ▶ **Example 4.7.** Let $A = \{1, 2, 3, 4, 5, 6\}$ and $B = \{2, 4, 6, 8, 10\}$.

Then $A - B = \{1, 3, 5\}$ and $B - A = \{8, 10\}$.   ◀ ◀ ◀

Definition 4.9. Power Set

Let S be a set. Then the power set of S, denoted by $P(S)$, is the set of all subsets of S.

▶ ▶ ▶ **Example 4.8.** The power set of {1,2,3} is

$$\{\varnothing, \{1\}, \{2\}, \{3\}, \{1, 2\}, \{1, 3\}, \{2, 3\}, \{1, 2, 3\}\}$$

Venn Diagrams in Python

The standard plotting package in python is matplotlib. Within matplotlib there is a sublibary **matplotlib_venn** that will produce rudimentary Venn diagrams of two and thee sets. The default labeling of these diagrams shows the number of items in each component of the diagram. The standard imports are

```
import numpy as np
import matplotlib.pyplot as plt
from matplotlib_venn import venn2, venn2_circles
from matplotlib_venn import venn3, venn3_circles
```

If we only want to do Venn diagrams of two sets, we only need to import **venn2** and **venn2_circles**, and if we only want to Venn diagrams of 3 sets and not two sets, we only need to import **venn3** and **venn3_circles**.

Next, suppose we define three different sets,

```
SomeGuys={"TOM",  "DICK","HARRY","JOHN","PAUL","CURLY"}
BeatlesPlusOne={"JOHN","PAUL","GEORGE","RINGO","CURLY"}
Stooges={"CURLY","MOE","LARRY"}
```

The bare-bones default Venn diagram of **Stooges** and **BeatlesPlusOne** looks like this:

```
v=venn2(subsets=(BeatlesPlusOne,Stooges))
```

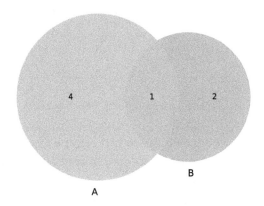

By default, the circles are filled with random colors, and the edges are not

---

drawn. The numbers give the number of elements in each set. The labels defalt to "A", "B", etc, in the order of the sets input.

The functions **venn2** and **venn3** draw the venn diagams as filled matplotlib patches. A desecription of the a **patch** object is well beyond the scope of this book. Suffice it to say that practically anything can be changed via low-level patch operations. If the return value is **v** then **v.patches** will produce a list of the patches produced by the function call. The functions **venn2_circles** and **venn3_circles** draw the edges of circles. An example follows.

```
v=venn3(subsets=(BeatlesPlusOne,Stooges,SomeGuys),
        set_labels=("Beatles", "Stooges", "Interlopers"))
for p in v.patches:
    p.set_color("white")
c=venn3_circles(subsets=(BeatlesPlusOne,Stooges,SomeGuys))
```

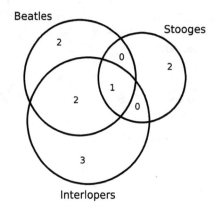

Set Identities

We mentioned earlier that in addition to element proofs there was a second method of proof about sets, called an identity proof. This is based on using a sequence of known identities about sets. This is useful because there are a large number of such identities that help us simplify complicated expressions about sets. Most of these expressions are very similar to logical identies that we have already seen previously. These identities can be derived using element proofs. Two examples of such identities are De Morgan's Laws of Sets. We call these particularly out as theorem **??** to illsutrate the poof.

Theorem 4.2. De Morgan's Laws of Sets

Let A, B be any sets. Then

$$\overline{A \cap B} = \overline{A} \cup \overline{B}$$
$$\overline{A \cup B} = \overline{A} \cap \overline{B}$$

Proof. We prove the first identity. The second is left for exercise 5. We need to show (a) that $\overline{A \cap B} \subseteq \overline{A} \cup \overline{B}$, and (b) that $\overline{A \cup B} \subseteq \overline{A \cap B}$.

Element proof of $\overline{A \cap B} \subseteq \overline{A} \cup \overline{B}$

1. Let $x \in \overline{A \cap B}$.
2. Then $x \notin A \cap B$ (definition of complement).
3. Then $\neg(x \in A \cap B)$ (definition of $\notin$).
4. Then $\neg((x \in A) \wedge (x \in B))$ (definition of intersection).
5. Then $\neg(x \in A) \vee \neg(x \in B)$ (De Morgan's law for logic).
6. Then $(x \notin A) \vee (x \notin B)$ (definition of $\notin$).
7. Then $(x \in \overline{A}) \vee (x \in \overline{B})$ (definition of complement).
8. Then $x \in (\overline{A} \cup \overline{B})$ (definintion of union).
9. Thus $\overline{A \cap B} \subseteq \overline{A} \cup \overline{B}$ (x is randomly chosen from $\overline{A \cap B}$)

Element proof of $\overline{A} \cup \overline{B} \subseteq \overline{A \cap B}$

1. Let $x \in \overline{A} \cup \overline{B}$.
2. Then $(x \in \overline{A}) \vee (x \in \overline{B})$ (definition of union).
3. Then $(x \notin A) \vee (x \notin B)$ (definition of complement).
4. Then $\neg(x \in A) \vee \neg(x \in B)$ (definition of $\notin$).
5. Then $\neg((x \in A) \wedge (x \in B))$ (De Morgan's law for logic).
6. Then $\neg(x \in A \cap B)$ (definition of intersection).
7. Then $x \notin A \cap B$ (definition of $\notin$).
8. Then $x \in \overline{A \cap B}$ (definition of complement).
9. Thus $\overline{A} \cup \overline{B} \subseteq \overline{A \cap B}$ (x was randomly chosen from $\overline{A} \cup \overline{B}$)

Since $\overline{A \cap B} \subseteq \overline{A} \cup \overline{B}$ and $\overline{A} \cup \overline{B} \subseteq \overline{A \cap B}$ we conclude that $\overline{A \cup B} =$

$\overline{A \cap B}$. □

Table 4.1. Set Identities

Here S,T,W are any sets; $\emptyset$ is the empy set; and $\mathbb{U}$ is the universal set.

Identity	Double Complement	Associative Law
$S \cup \emptyset = S$	$\overline{(\overline{S})} = S$	$S \cup (T \cup W) = (S \cup T) \cup W$
$S \cap \mathbb{U} = S$	**Complement**	$S \cap (T \cap W) = (S \cap T) \cap W$
Domination	$S \cap \overline{S} = \emptyset$	**De Morgan's Law**
$S \cap \emptyset = \emptyset$	$S \cup \overline{S} = \mathbb{U}$	$\overline{S \cap T} = \overline{S} \cup \overline{T}$
$S \cup \mathbb{U} = \mathbb{U}$	**Commutative Law**	$\overline{S \cup T} = \overline{S} \cap \overline{T}$
Idempotent Laws	$S \cup T = T \cup S$	**Absorption**
$S \cup S = S$	$S \cap T = T \cap S$	$S \cup (S \cap T) = S$
$S \cap S = S$		$S \cap (S \cup T) = S$

Distributive Law
$$S \cup (T \cap W) = (S \cup T) \cap (S \cup W)$$
$$S \cap (T \cup W) = (S \cap T) \cup (S \cap W)$$

Tuples and Products

Definition 4.10. Ordered Pair

An **ordered pair** is a pair of items or objects, such as a and b, in a specific order, written as (a, b).

An **n-tuple** (sometimes just called a **tuple**) is an ordered collection of n (at least 2) objects in a specified order, such as (a, b, c) or (p, q, r, s, t).

The properties of an ordered pair (or a tuple) depend not only on the items in the pair (or tuple), but also in their ordering. Thus if $a \neq b$ then the pairs (a, b) and (b, a) are different. We say two pairs (or tuples) are equal if they have the same items at the same location:

$$(a, b) = (c, d)$$

means that $a = c$ and $b = d$. Thus while the sets $\{1, 2\} = \{2, 1\}$ are equal, the order pairs $(1, 2)$ and $(2, 1)$ are not equal. Shorter tuples are sometimes referenced, e.g., as **triples** (for a 3-tuple), **quadruple** (a 4-tuple), etc.

Ch. 4. Sets

Definition 4.11. Cartesian Product

The **Cartesian Product** of two sets A and B is the set of ordered pairs

$$A \times B = \{(a, b) | (a \in A) \wedge (b \in B)\}$$

The Cartesian product of the sets $A_1, A_2, \ldots, A_n$ is the set of tuples

$$A_1 \times A_2 \times \cdots \times A_n = \{(a_1, a_2, \ldots, a_n) | (a_1 \in A_1) \wedge (a_2 \in A_2) \wedge$$
$$\cdots \wedge (a_n \in A_n)\}$$

Each element in the Cartesian product is obtained by picking one item from each set, in the same order. Then the Cartesian product is the collection of all possible tuples picked in this manner.

▶ ▶ ▶ **Example 4.9.** Let $A = \{10, 20\}$ and $B = \{x, y)\}$. Then

$$A \times B = \{10, 20\} \times \{x, y\}$$
$$= \{(10, x), (10, y), (20, x), (20, y)\}$$

◀ ◀ ◀

▶ ▶ ▶ **Example 4.10.** The lunch special at Fred's Diner allows you to pick one starter (soup or salad), one main item (hambuger or hot dog), and one drink (cola, coffee, or tea).

Let $A = \{\text{soup}, \text{salad}\}$, $B = \{\text{hamburger}, \text{hot dog}\}$, and $C = \{\text{cola}, \text{coffee}, \text{tea}\}$. Then a single possible meal is denoted by a tuple (a, b, c), where $a \in A$, $b \in B$, and $c \in C$. The set of all possible meal combinations is given by

$$A \times B \times C = \{\text{soup}, \text{salad}\} \times \{\text{hamburger}, \text{hot dog}\} \times \{\text{cola}, \text{coffee}, \text{tea}\}$$
$$= \{(\text{soup, hamburger, cola}), (\text{soup, hamburger,coffee}),$$
$$(\text{soup, hamburger, tea}), (\text{salad, hamburger, cola}),$$
$$(\text{salad, hamburger, coffee}), (\text{salad, hamburger, tea}),$$
$$(\text{soup, hot dog, cola}), (\text{soup, hot dog,coffee}),$$
$$(\text{soup, hot dog, tea}), (\text{salad, hot dog, cola}),$$
$$(\text{salad, hot dog, coffee}), (\text{salad, hot dog, tea})\}$$

◀ ◀ ◀

Tuples in Python

A tuple is expressed in python as a sequence of objects separated by commas and enclosed by parenthesis. They are similar to python lists in that the objects may be accesed by index. They are different in that tuples are considered immutable objects in python, namely, once a variable is assigned a tuple value, the parts of the tuple may not be changed. For example, suppose that

```
x=(1,2)
y=[1,2]
```

Then while the following is perfectly valid:

```
y[1]=5
print(y)
```

```
[1,5]
```

any attempt to do the same thing to a tuple will give an error:

```
x[1]=5
```

```
-----------------------------------------------------------------
---------------
TypeError
Traceback (most recent call last)
<ipython-input-57-0586ef3e8b02> in <module>()
----> 1 x[1]=5

TypeError: 'tuple' object does not support item assignment
```

The cartesian product of two sets can be obtained using the function **itertools.product**.

```
S={1,2,3}
T={"a","b"}
set(itertools.product(S,T))
```

```
{(1, 'a'), (1, 'b'), (2, 'a'), (2, 'b'), (3, 'a'), (3, 'b')}
```

Cartesian products of a set with itself n times can be obtained using the **repeat** keyword, for example **set(itertools.product(1,0, repeat=3)** returns the set { **(0, 0, 0)**, **(0, 0, 1)**, **(0, 1, 0)**, **(0, 1, 1)**, **(1, 0, 0)**, **(1, 0, 1)**, **(1, 1, 0)**, **(1, 1, 1)** }. An example of its use was given in the progam that printed truth tables on page 10.

Exercises

1. Suppose that $A = \mathbb{Z}^+$,
   $B = \{n \in \mathbb{Z} | 0 \leqslant n \leqslant 100\}$, and
   $C = \{100, 200, 300, 400, 500\}$.

   a) Is $B \subseteq A$?
   b) Is C a proper subset of A?
   c) Do C and B have at least one element in common?
   d) Is $C \subseteq B$?
   e) What is the cardinality of C?

2. Determine the truth value of each of the following:

   a) $2 \in \{1, 2, 3\}$
   b) $\{2\} \in \{1, 2, 3\}$
   c) $2 \subseteq \{1, 2, 3\}$
   d) $\{2\} \subseteq \{1, 2, 3\}$
   e) $\{2\} \subseteq \{\{1\}, \{2\}\}$
   f) $\{2\} \in \{\{1\}, \{2\}\}$

3. Let $A = \{1, 2, 3\}$ and $B = \{4, 5\}$.

   a) Find $A \times B$
   b) Find $B \times A$
   c) Find $B \times B$
   d) How many elements do each of the above sets have?

4. Describe $\mathbb{R} \times \mathbb{R}$ using set builder notation.

5. Prove De Morgan's second law for sets: $\overline{A \cup B} = \overline{A} \cap \overline{B}$.

6. Prove each of the remaining identities in table 4.1 using an element argument.

7. What is the power set of $\varnothing$?

8. What is the power set of $\{\varnothing\}$?

9. Find the power set of $\{apples, oranges\}$.

10. What do you think is the cardinality of the power set of a set of cardinality n?

11. Let $S = \{k^2 | k \in \mathbb{Z}^+\}$. Is the cardinality of S the same, greater then, or less than the cardinality of $\mathbb{Z}^+$

5. Direct Proof and Number Theory

In a direct proof we use a straightforward chain of inference to reach our goal. Each step must be justified by things that have been previously proven, either by an earlier step in the proof, or in any previously stated definition, theorem, axiom, postulate, etc. In this chapter we will introduce some basic results of number theory and prove or apply them using the method of direct proof. We will build upon these results in subsequent chapters.

We asume the student is already familiar with the integers (denoted by $\mathbb{Z}$), the positive integers (the set $\mathbb{Z}^+ = \{1, 2, 3, \dots\}$) and the set of of non-negative integer (or natural numbers, $\mathbb{N} = \{0, 1, 2, 3, \dots\}$). For the most part we will accept that the student is familiar with the basic properties of arithmetic and alegebra, and is familiar with the distinction between the integers and the real numbers (denoted by the set $\mathbb{R}$.

We will all take the following statement of the closure of the integers as an accepted fact.

Axiom 5.1. Closure of Integers

The integers are closed under addition, subtraction, and multiplication. More specifically, if $x, y \in \mathbb{Z}$, then $x + y \in \mathbb{Z}$, $x - y \in \mathbb{Z}$, and $xy \in \mathbb{Z}$.

Note that closure under subtraction does not apply to $\mathbb{Z}^+$ or $\mathbb{N}$, but the positive and non-negative integers remain closed under addition and multiplication.

The reason why integers are closed under three operations (addition, subtraction, and multiplication) but not the fourth (division) is because when we divide integers (except for division by zero), we get fractions. Fractions composed of integers divided by other (non-zero) integers are called **rational** numbers.

Definition 5.1. Rational Number

We say that a number x is **rational** if there exists integers p, q, with $q \neq 0$, such that $x = p/q$. The set of all rational numbers is denoted by the special symbol $\mathbb{Q}$.

If no such integers exist, then x is said to be **irrational**.

Examples of irrational numbers include π, e (the base of the natural logarithms), and $\sqrt{2}$. In fact, if n is any positive integer that is not the square of a perfect integer, then $\sqrt{n}$ is irrational. We will prove that $\sqrt{2}$ is irrational in chapter 9. Examples of rational numbers include all integers, such as 17, 42/3, 3/5, and -32/3. Furthermore, all repeating decimals are integers.

▶ ▶ ▶ **Example 5.1.** Show that $x = 0.372372372...$ is rational. (the overline means that the 372 is repeated over and over again).

$$x = 0.372372\overline{372}$$
$$1000x = 372.372372\overline{372} \qquad \text{multiply by 1000}$$
$$999x = 372 \qquad \text{Subtract 1st line from 2nd line}$$
$$x = 372/999 \qquad \text{Divide by 999}$$

Thus $0.372372\overline{372} = 372/999$ is a rational number.

Theorem 5.2.

The sum of two rational numbers is a rational number

Proof. We need to show that the sum of any two randomly chosen rational numbers is also a rational numbers. Formally, $(\forall x, y \in \mathbb{Q})(x + y \in \mathbb{Q})$. Here we present a direct proof with the steps in the proof sequentially numbered. This is not necessary, but it helps to illustrate the concept. Each numbered item depends only on conclusions of earlier steps, or on previously stated theorems, axioms, definitions, etc. Eventually we will replace the numbered steps with paragraphs, and then sentences.

1. Let $x, y \in \mathbb{Q}$. We need to show that $x + y \in \mathbb{Q}$.

2. Since $x \in \mathbb{Q}$, then there exist integers a, b with $b \neq 0$, such that $x = a/b$ (by definition 1).

3. Since $y \in \mathbb{Q}$, then there exist integers c, d with $d \neq 0$, such that $y = c/d$ (by definition 1).

4. Adding together $x + y$ and doing some algebra,

$$x + y = \frac{a}{b} + \frac{c}{d} = \frac{ad + bc}{bd}$$

5. Since the integers are closed under multiplication (Axiom 5.1) and addition, the combination $p = ad + bc \in \mathbb{Z}$.

6. Since the integers are closed under multiplicaton (Axiom 5.1), the product $q = bd \in Z$.

7. By the zero-product property (Axiom 5.3), $q \neq 0$.

8. By substitution, $x + y = p/q$, where $p, q \in \mathbb{Z}$ and $q \neq 0$. Hence by definition 1, $x + y \in \mathbb{Q}$, which was what we wanted to prove.

Therefore the sum of two rational numbers is a rational number. □

Another fact that we will accept without proof is the zero product property.

Axiom 5.3. Zero Product Property

Suppose $x, y \in \mathbb{R}$ such that $x \neq 0$ and $y \neq 0$. Then $xy \neq 0$.

The idea of **divisibility** formalizes that concept that some integers will "evenly" divide into other integers without anything left over (no **remainder**). The word "evenly" can be a bit confusing here. We have used it to mean "nothing left over," as in "split the tab evenly between the three of us," or "spread the batter out evenly on the bottom of the cake pan." However, one should really try to avoid the word "even" in all of its forms when discussing divisibility to avoid confusion with even numbers, which are numbers that are divisible by two.

Definition 5.2. Divisibility

An integer n is **divisible** by an integer d if there is an integer k such that $dk = n$. We write $d|n$, and say, equivalently:

- d divides n
- d is a factor of n
- n is divisible by d
- n is a multiple of d

Definition 5.3. Even Number

An integer n is **even** if $2|n$. Thus when n is even, there is some integer k such that $n = 2k$.

If an integer is not even, it is said to be **odd**. When n is odd, there is some integer k such that $n = 2k + 1$.

Theorem 5.4. Sum of Even Numbers

The sum of two even numbers is an even number.

Proof. By direct proof:

1. Let p and q be even integers.

2. Then by the definition of an even number, there exist integers j and k such that $p = 2j$ and $q = 2k$.

3. Adding them together and factoring,

$$p + q = 2j + 2k = 2(j + k) = 2m$$

where $m = j + k$.

4. The number $m = j + k$ is an integer because the integers are closed under addition (axiom 5.1).

5. Since $p + q = 2m$, we have $2|(p + q)$. So $p + q$ is even.

Thus the sum of two evens is even. □

Theorem 5.5.

If x and y are positive integers such that $x|y$ then $x \leqslant y$.

Proof. Let $x, y \in \mathbb{Z}^+$, where $x|y$.

1. By the definition of divisibility (def. 2), since $x|y$, there exists an integer $k \in \mathbb{Z}$ such that $y = kx$.

2. Since $x \neq 0$ we can divide by x, giving $k = y/x$.

3. Since the quotient of positive integers must be a positive number, $k \geqslant 1$.

4. By substitution, $y/x \geqslant 1$ or $y \geqslant x$.

Thus $(\forall x, y \in \mathbb{Z}^+)(x|y) \Rightarrow (x \leqslant y)$. □

Theorem 5.6. Transitivity of Divisibility

If $x|y$ and $y|z$ then $x|z$.

Proof. Let x, y, and z be integers such that $x|y$ and $y|z$.

1. Since $x|y$ there is an integer p such that $y = px$ (definition of divisibility).
2. Since $y|z$ there is an integer q such that $z = qy$ (definition of divisibility).
3. By substution $z = qy = qpx = kx$ where $k = xy$.
4. By the closure of the integers under multiplication, k is an integer.
5. Since $z = kx$ where $k \in \mathbb{Z}$, by the definition of divisibility, we have $x|z$.

Thus divisibility is transitive. □

Exercises

1. Prove that if you double a rational number, the result is a new rational number.

2. Prove the following: if $x \in \mathbb{Q}$, the $5x^2 - 12x + 17 \in \mathbb{Q}$.

3. Determine whether or not each of the following are true. If so, write the statement in $d|n$ notation.

a) 21 is divisible by 3
b) 45 is a multiple of -16
c) -60 is a multiple of 15
d) 5 divides 45
e) 6 is a factor of 54

4. Prove or disprove each of the following statements.

a) Suppose $k \neq 0$. Then $k|0$.
b) Suppose $k \neq 0$. Then $0|k$.
c) Let p, q be any integers. Then $7|(7p + 7q)$.
d) $(x, y \in \mathbb{Z}) \Rightarrow (15|30xy)$.

6. Proof by Cases

We often need to prove things that depend on the **absolute value** of a number. The absolute value itself is a classic example of a definition that has two different cases. Although you are probably already familiar with the absolute value, we present the formal definition here.

Definition 6.1. Absolute Value

Let $x \in \mathbb{R}$. Then the **Absolute Value** of x, written as $|x|$, is given by

$$|x| = \begin{cases} x & \text{if } x \geq 0 \\ -x & \text{if } x < 0 \end{cases}$$

We can give the absolute value a geometric interpretation: it measures the magnitude of the distance of x, as measured along the x axis, from the origin. Hence it is always positive or zero, and is zero only when $x = 0$.

We use cases to prove properties of the absolute value. Within the proofs, the two cases will be based on the two cases of the definition: $x \geq 0$ and $x < 0$.

Theorem 6.1.

For all real numbers x, $-|x| \leq x \leq |x|$.

Proof. Either $x \geq 0$ or $x < 0$.

$\underline{x \geq 0}$:

1. Since $x \geq 0$ then by definition of absolute value, $|x| = x \geq 0$.
2. Therefore $-|x| = -x \leq 0$.
3. Hence $-|x| \leq -x < 0 \leq x \leq |x|$
4. Simplifying gives the required result $-|x| \leq x \leq |x|$.

$\underline{x < 0}$

1. By definition of absolute value, $|x| = -x < 0$
2. Multiplying by -1 gives $-|x| = x > 0$
3. Since $-|x| = x$, then also $-|x| \leqslant x$
4. Since $x < 0$ and $|x| > 0$, $x < 0 < |x| \leqslant |x|$
5. Combining step 3 and step 4 $-|x| \leqslant x \leqslant |x|$ as required.

$\square$

All real numbers are either positive, negative, or zero. This principle is known as the principle of trichotomy of real numbers. Sometimes we will find it convenient (or necessary) to use trichotomy in a proof by cases.

Definition 6.2. Trichotomy of Real Numbers

For any real number x, by the principle of trichotomy, one of the following three cases must hold: $x < 0$, $x = 0$, or $x > -$.

Theorem 6.2.

For all real numbers x, $|-x| = |x|$

Proof. We will consider three possible cases: $x < 0$, $x = 0$, or $x > 0$.

If $\underline{x < 0}$:

1. Since $x < 0$, $|x| = -x$ (def. of absolute value)
2. Since $x < 0$, $-x > 0$ (multiply by -1)
3. $|-x| = -x$ (by def. of absolute value and step 2)
4. Hence $|-x| = |x|$ (substitute step 1 into step 3)

If $\underline{x = 0}$:

1. Since $x = 0$, $|x| = x = 0$ (def. of absolute value)
2. Since $x = 0$, $-x = 0$ (multiply by -1)
3. Hence $|-x| = |0| = 0$ (step 2 and def. of absolute value)

---

4. Hence $|-x| = |x|$ (combine steps 1 and 3)

If $x > 0$:

1. Since $x > 0$ then $|x| = x$ (def. of absolute value)
2. Since $x > 0$ then $-x < 0$ (multiply by -1)
3. Hence $|-x| = -(-x) = x$ (def. of absolute value, step 2)
4. Hence $|-x| = |x|$ (combine steps 1 and 3)

Thus for all real numbers x, $|x| = |-x|$. □

Theorem 6.3. Triangle Inequality for Real Numbers

Let x, y be any real numbers. Then $|x + y| \leqslant |x| + |y|$.

Proof. Either $x + y \geqslant 0$ or $x + y < 0$.

If $x + y \geqslant 0$:

1. Since $x + y \geqslant 0$, then by definition of absolute value, $|x + y| = x + y$.
2. By theorem 6.1, $x \leqslant |x|$.
3. By theorem 6.1, $y \leqslant |y|$.
4. Substituting the results of steps 2 and 3 into the result of step 1 gives $|x + y| \leqslant |x| + |y|$, which is the desired result.

If $x + y < 0$:

1. By definition of absolute value, $|x + y| = -(x + y)$.
2. Hence $|x + y| = (-x) + (-y)$ (algebra)
3. By theorem 6.1, $(-x) \leqslant |-x|$
4. By theorem 6.1, $(-y) \leqslant |-y|$
5. By substitution $|x + y| \leqslant |-x| + |-y|$
6. By theorem 6.2, $|-x| = |x|$ and $|-y| = |y|$
7. By subsitution $|x + y| \leqslant |x| + |y|$, which is the desired result.

□

Often in proofs we are required to show either the **existence** or the **uniqueness** of some quantity. To prove existence we need to show that at least one of that item exists. Often we will actually construct the item, and show that it works. For example, we may be required to prove a statement like "There is a unique positive integer that solves the equation $x - 4 = 0$." To prove the existence of this unique positive integer, it is sufficient (though perhaps not very elegant) to pull the number 4 out of the air, plug it into the equation, and show that it works. Uniquenes is harder to prove - we need to show that if we pull any other number x' out of the air, and plug it into the equation, we must also get $x' = 4$. Most frequently this is proven by contradiction, which will be examined in more detail in chapter 9. Sometimes the very statement of existence in the theorem itself is subtle we may not even realize that we need to prove existence at all!. Theorem 6.4 is an example of this.

Theorem 6.4.

The only divisors of 1 are 1 and -1.

Proof. This brief theorem states that the only divisors of 1 are 1 and -1. Hence two divisors exists, so we need first to show that (a) these are the correct divisors (existence); and then (b) prove their uniqueness.

To prove existence:

1. Since $1 \cdot 1 = 1$, 1 is a divisor of 1 (definition 5.2).
2. Since $(-1) \cdot (-1) = 1$, -1 is a divisor of 1 (definition 5.2).

To prove uniqueness:

1. Suppose that m is any divisor (not necessarily 1 or -1) of 1.
2. Then there is some number $n \in \mathbb{Z}$ such that $mn = 1$.
3. By the properties of real numbers, since $mn = 1 > 0$, either both m and n are positive (case 1) or both m and n are negative. (If one is postive and the other is negative, then their product would be negative).

Consider case 1 (both m and n are postive).

1. By theorem 5.5.5, $m|1 \Rightarrow m \leqslant 1$.
2. Since $m \in \mathbb{Z}$ and $m > 0$, $m \geqslant 1$.

---

3. Since $m \leqslant 1$ and $m \geqslant 1$ the only possibility is that $m = 1$.

Consider case 2 (both m and n are negative).

1. Because $m < 0$ and $n < 0$, we know that $-m > 0$ and $-n > 0$.
2. Multiplying, $(-m)(-n) = (-1)(m)(-1)(n) = mn = 1$
3. Therefore $-m|1$ by the definintion of divisibility, where $-m > 0$ is a positive divisor of 1.
4. By theorem 5.5.5, $-m \leqslant 1$.
5. Combining the last two results gives $-m = 1$ or $m = -1$

Therefore the only two divisors of 1 are 1 and -1.   □

Prime and Composite Numbers

Note that when we define primes, 1 is not included, and we only include positive integers in the definition.

Definition 6.3. Prime Number

An integer $n > 1$ is said to be **prime**, or a **prime number**, if and only if its only positive divisors are 1 and n.

An integer that is not prime is called **composite**.

▶ ▶ ▶ **Example 6.1.** 17 is prime because its only divisors are 1 and 17.

18 is composite because it has factors of 1,2,3,6,9, and 18.

Theorem 6.5.

If n is composite then it has a least two positive factors p, q, such that $1 < p < n$ and $1 < q < n$.

Theorem 6.6.

Every integer $n > 1$ is either prime or composite.

Proof. Let $n > 1$ be an integer.

1. Consider all the possible ordered pairs (p, q) such that $pq = n$.
2. Since $p|n$, we know that $1 \leqslant p \leqslant n$.
3. Since $q|n$, we know that $1 \leqslant q \leqslant n$
4. We can identify at least two such ordered pairs: $(n, 1)$ and $(n, 1)$. We consideres the following two cases:

Case 1. $(n, 1)$ and $(n, 1)$ are the only such ordered pairs.
         In this case, n and 1 the factors of n, hence n is prime.
Case 2. There are other ordered pairs besides $(n, 1)$ and $(n, 1)$.

1. Let (p, q) be one such pair of factors with $n = pq$ such that $n \neq p$ and $n \neq q$.
2. We must have $1 < p < n$. Otherwise we would have $n = pq \geqslant nq > n$.
3. Similarly, $1 < q < n$.
4. Thus n is composite because it has factors that are distinct from both 1 and n.

Thus every integer either prime or composite. $\square$

Theorem 6.7. Divisibility by a Prime

Every integer $n > 1$ is divisible by a prime number.

Proof. Let $n > 1$ be a positive integer. Either n is prime (case 1) or n is not prime (case 2).

Consider case 1 (n is prime).

1. Since n is prime, it can be written as $n = 1 \cdot n$, where n is prime.
2. Hence n is divisible by a prime.

Now consider case 2 (n is not a prime).

1. Since n is not prime, it must have factors $r_0, s_0 \in \mathbb{Z}$ that are different from 1 and n, i.e.,

$$r_0 s_0 = n, \; 1 < r_0 <, \; 1 < s_0 < n$$

2. If r_0 is a prime number, then $r_0 | n$ and the proof is finished.
3. If r_0 is not a prime number, then it must be possible to factor it, so that

$$r_0 = r_1 s_1, \; 1 < r_1 < r_0, \; 1 < s_1 < r_0$$

4. If r_1 is a prime number, then we are finished because $n = r_1 s_1 s_0$ so $r_1 | n$.
5. If r_1 is not prime, we can factor it as

$$r_1 = r_2 s_2, \; 1 < r_2 < r_1, \; 1 < s_2 < r_1$$

6. Keep repeating the process, generating a sequence of successively smaller r_j, with

$$1 < r_{j+1} < r_j < r_0$$

Since the r_j are getting smaller and the number is finite, the sequence will end, either at a prime number, or at 2, which is prime.

$\square$

We will see later (theorem 9.4) that every integer has a unique prime factorization

$$p = \sum_{j=1}^{k} p_j^{\epsilon_j} = p_1^{\epsilon_1} p_2^{\epsilon_2} \cdots p_k^{\epsilon_k}$$

where $p_1, p_2, \ldots, p_k$ are prime. Here $\epsilon_1, \epsilon_2, \ldots, \epsilon_k$ are positive integers (called the multiplicities). The **standard form** is to arrange all the prime factors in increasing numerical order.

Definition 6.4. Standard Factored Form

Let n be a prime number. Then the prime factorization

$$p = \sum_{j=1}^{k} p_j^{\epsilon_j} = p_1^{\epsilon_1} p_2^{\epsilon_2} \cdots p_k^{\epsilon_k}$$

with prime factors p_j and corresponding multiplicities ϵ_j, it is said to be in **standard factored form** if

$$p_1 < p_2 < \cdots < p_k$$

i.e., if the factors are arranged in increasing numerical order.

▶ ▶ ▶ **Example 6.2.** The standard factorization 358 can be factored is $358 = 2^3 \cdot 3^2 \cdot 5$.

Other correct factorizations include $358 = 5 \cdot 2^3 \cdot 3^2$.   ◀ ◀ ◀

▶ ▶ ▶ **Example 6.3.** What is the least postive integer x such that $2^3 \cdot 3 \cdot 5 \cdot x$ is a perfect square?

For an integer to be a perfect square, all of the exponents in the prime factorization must be even.

We need one factor of 2, one factor of 3, and one factor of 5 to get even exponents on all the prime factors.

Hence $x = 2 \cdot 3 \cdot 5 = 30$.

The actual perfect square is $2^3 \cdot 3 \cdot 5 \cdot 30 = 3600$.

The prime factorization is $2^4 \cdot 3^2 \cdot 5^2$. The square root is $2^2 \cdot 3 \cdot 5 = 60$.

A Algorithm for Finding Primes

One of the oldest method for making a list of all the prime numbers smaller than some integer N is called the **Sieve of Eratosthones**. The idea is pretty simple:

1. Make a list of all the numbers from 2 to N
2. Cross off all the multiples of 2.
3. Find the smallest number that remains (3).
4. Cross off all the multiples of 3.
5. Find the smallest nuumber that remains (5)
6. Cross off all the multiples of 5.
7. Repeat (crossing off) until you get to the square root of N.
8. Anything that is left is prime.

To implement this algorithm, we start with an array all **True**'s. As we cross things on, we turn a **True** to a **False**. When we implement this, we note that we only have to check the factors that are smaller than or equal to $\sqrt{n}$. This is because corresponding to any factor that is larger than $\sqrt{n}$ there must be another factor that is smaller than $\sqrt{n}$. When we are done, we need to determine the index of all the remaining **True**'s in the array. We do this with Python's built in **enumerate** function, which returns a generator with successive ordered pairs of (i, x), where i is the index and x is the value. We use generator comprehension to produce the entire sequence of values.

Here is a straightforward implementation in Python:

```
from math import sqrt
def sieve_of_eratosthenes(n):
    # Returns the prime numbers up through n
    flags = (n-1) * [True]
    upperbound = int(sqrt(n))+1
    for factor in range(2, upperbound): # check every factor
        for k in range(2*factor, n+1, factor):
            # multipes of the factor, like 6,9,12,15,...
            flags[k-2]=False
    # pick out the ones that are not crossed off
    # enumerate starts at 0 so add 2 to the index
    primes = (x+2 for x,y in enumerate(flags) if y==True)
    return(primes)
```

To pretty-print, say, all of the primes under 1000,

```
p=sieve_of_eratosthones(1000)
j=0
for x in p:
    print ("{:5d}".format(x), end="")
    j+=1
    if j%10==0:
        print()
```

```
    2    3    5    7   11   13   17   19   23   29
   31   37   41   43   47   53   59   61   67   71
   73   79   83   89   97  101  103  107  109  113
  127  131  137  139  149  151  157  163  167  173
  179  181  191  193  197  199  211  223  227  229
  233  239  241  251  257  263  269  271  277  281
  283  293  307  311  313  317  331  337  347  349
  353  359  367  373  379  383  389  397  401  409
  419  421  431  433  439  443  449  457  461  463
  467  479  487  491  499  503  509  521  523  541
  547  557  563  569  571  577  587  593  599  601
  607  613  617  619  631  641  643  647  653  659
  661  673  677  683  691  701  709  719  727  733
  739  743  751  757  761  769  773  787  797  809
  811  821  823  827  829  839  853  857  859  863
  877  881  883  887  907  911  919  929  937  941
  947  953  967  971  977  983  991  997
```

Exercises

1. Let k be an integer. Prove by cases that $3k^2 + 4k + 8$ is even.

2. Let k be an integer. Prove by cases that $k + k^2$ is even.

3. Let k be an integer. Prove by cases that whenever k^2 is divided by 5 using integer division, the remainder is either 1 or 4.

4. Show that $k^5 - k$ is divisible by 3 for any positive integer k. Hint: Factor $K^5 - k$ and consider all possible remainders when k is divided by 3.

5. Show that the product of two consecutive integers is even.

6. Show that the square of any odd integer has the form $8k + 1$ for some integer k. Hint: let m be odd and consider all possible remainders after m is divided by 4.

7. A brute-force algorithm for determining if a x is prime would check all integers less than or equal to $\sqrt{x}$ to see if they were factors of x. Implement a brute force algorithm for the primes and compare its speed to the sieve of Erasthones.

8. Is it possible to write a function to determine all the primes between n and m, where $n < m$, without first finding all the primes that are smaller than n?

9. Write a function to find a prime factorization of an integer.

10. Write a function to find the prime factorization of an integer and convert it to standard form.

7. Disproof by Counterexample

Disproof by counterexample is used to **disprove universally quantified statements**. It is based on the following equivalence:

$$\neg(\forall x)(P(x)) \equiv (\exists x)(\neg P(x))$$

Therefore single counterexample is sufficient to disprove the statement $(\forall x)(P(x))$. If we can find a number a such such that $\neg P(a)$, then we have demonstrated that $(\exists a)(\neg P(a))$, and therefore disproven the statement $(\forall x)(P(x))$.

> ▶ ▶ ▶ **Example 7.1.** Use a counterexample to disprove the following statement: for all positive integers n, the number $n^2 - n + 41$ is prime.
>
> *Proof.* Consider the formula for $n = 41$:
>
> $$n^2 - n + 41 = 41^2 - 41 + 41 = 41^2$$
>
> Since $41^2 = 41 \cdot 41$, it is not a prime number. Hence the statement is **False**. □

◀ ◀ ◀

Disproof by counterexample is closely related to the **proof of an existentially quantified (there exists) statement** by a single example. While it only takes a single example to disprove a universally quantified (for all) statement, it also only takes a single example to prove an existentially quantified statement.

Let us define the statement

$$P(n) = \text{``the number } n^2 - n + 41 \text{ is always prime''}$$

Then we can construct both a universal statement

$$(\forall n)(P(n))$$

which we disproved in example 1. The negation of this statement is

$$(\exists n)(\neg P(n))$$

But $\neg P(n)$ is the statement that there is a some number such that $n^2 - n + 41$ is not prime. Thus we can also use a single example to prove an existentially quantified statement.

▶ ▶ ▶ **Example 7.2.** Use an single example to prove existence in the following statement: there is an integer n, such that the number $n^2 - n + 41$ is not prime.

Proof. Consider the formula for $n = 41$:

$$n^2 - n + 41 = 41^2 - 41 + 41 = 41^2$$

Since $41^2 = 41 \cdot 41$, it is not a prime number. Hence the statement is **True**. □

 ◀ ◀ ◀

The proof of the existentially quantified statement by example is based on the equivalence

$$\neg(\exists x)(Q(x)) \equiv (\forall x)(\neg P(x))$$

This balances the statement we made at the beginning of the chapter.

Exercises

Prove the following existential statements by coming up with an example.

1. There exists an integer k such that $\sqrt{k}$ is an odd integer.

2. For any odd integer k, then k is the difference between two perfect squares.

Disprove the following univseral statements by finding a counterexample.

3. Let S be the set of all positive even integers. Then $S \cap \mathbb{Z} = \varnothing$.

4. There are no irrational numbers.

5. Let k be an integer. Then $\sqrt{k}$ is irrational.

Ch. 7. Disproof by Counterexample

8. Proof by Contraposition

The methods of proof by contraposition and proof by contradiction are closely related by they are different, and students often get them related. We will demonstrate their use by diving into some properties of numbers. Since we are not developing a rigorous foundation of discrete mathematics, rather than starting from the basics, we will, at times, use some known facts that students are already familiar with. The purpose here is primarily to get used to proving things, and not learnign about integers and such.

To prove a statment $P(x)$ by contradiction:

1. Suppose the statement to be proven is false, i.e., $\neg P(x)$

2. Show that this assumption leads logically to a contradiction.

3. Conclude that the statement to be proven in true.

Theorem 8.1.

There is no greatest integer.

Proof. Suppose that there is a largest integer. Call it N.

The by definition of "largest",

$$(\forall n \in \mathbb{Z})(N \geqslant n) \tag{8.1}$$

Let $m = N + 1$. Since $N \in \mathbb{Z}$, then $m \in \mathbb{Z}$, because the integers are closed under addtion.

But $m > N$, and thus we have produced an integer that is larger than the largest integer. This contraducts the statement (8.1). Hence the earlier assumption, that there that there is a largest integer, must be false. Thus there is no largest integer. $\square$

Theorem 8.2.

No integer can be both even and odd.

Proof. Prove by contradiction. Suppose that there is at least one integer $n \in \mathbb{Z}$ that is both even and odd.

Since n is even, $\exists k \in \mathbb{Z}$ such that $n = 2k$.

Since n is odd, $\exists p \in \mathbb{Z}$ such that $n = 2p + 1$.

Equating the last two expressions, $2k = 2p + 1$ for some $k, p \in \mathbb{Z}$. Rearranging,

$$2k - 2p = 1$$
$$2(k - p) = 1$$
$$k - p = \frac{1}{2}$$

Since the integers are closed under subtraction, $k - p \in \mathbb{Z}$. Since the left hand side of the equation is an integer, so is the right hand side. Thus $1/2 \in \mathbb{Z}$. This contradicts the known fact, that $1/2 \notin \mathbb{Z}$

We may deduce from this contradiction that we have made an incorrect assumption. Our only assumption was that there is at least one integer that is both even and odd is false.

Hence there are no integers that are both even and odd. $\square$

Theorem 8.3.

The sum of a rational number and an irrational number is irrational.

Proof. Proof by contradiction. Suppose that $\exists r \in \mathbb{Q}$ and $\exists x \in \mathbb{R}$, where x is irrational, such that $r + x \in \mathbb{Q}$.

Since $r \in \mathbb{Q}$, by definition of rational, $\exists m, n \in \mathbb{Z}$ such that

$$r = \frac{m}{n}, \text{ with } n \neq 0$$

Since (by assumption) $r + x \in \mathbb{Q}$, $\exists a, b \in \mathbb{Z}$, with $b \neq 0$, such that

$$r + x = \frac{a}{b}$$

By substitution,

$$\frac{m}{n} + x = \frac{a}{b}$$

Subtracting m/n from both sides of the equation,

$$x = \frac{a}{b} - \frac{m}{n} = \frac{an - mb}{nb}$$

Since the integers are closed under multiplication and subtraction, the numerator is an integer. Since n and b are both non-zero integers, their product is a nonzero integer. Hence x is the quotient of two integers. This means $x \in \mathbb{Q}$, i.e., it is rational.

But we assumed that x is irrational. This is a contradiction. Hence the original assumption (our only asusmption) is incorrect. Thus there is no possible combination of rational numbers and irrational numbers that sum to a rational numbers.

Hence the sum of a rational and an irrational is irrational. □

A proof by contraposition is based on the fact that an "if-then" statement such as $P \Rightarrow Q$ is equivalent to its contrapositive $\neg Q \Rightarrow \neg P$. Proving the contrapositive is true is a good as proving that the original statement is true.

To prove a statement R, where,

$$R : (\forall x \in D)(P(x) \Rightarrow Q(x))$$

using the method of proof by contraposition,

1. Rewrite R as its contrapositive S:

$$S : (\forall x \in D)(\neg Q(x) \Rightarrow \neg P(x))$$

2. Prove that S is **True**:

   a) Let $x \in D$ such that $\neg Q(x)$

b) Show that $P(x)$ is **False** follows as a logical consequence of this assumption.

c) Conclude that $\neg Q \Rightarrow \neg P$.

3. Since $S \equiv R$, conclude that R is true.

Theorem 8.4.

If n^2 is even then n is even.

Proof. Formally, the expression to be proven is

$$(\forall n \in \mathbb{Z})(P(n) \Rightarrow Q(n))$$

where

$$P(n) : n^2 \text{ is even}$$
$$Q(n) : n \text{ is even}$$

The contrapositive of the statement we want to prove is

$$(\forall n \in \mathbb{Z})(\neg Q(n) \Rightarrow \neg P(n))$$

Confusing Point for Students: Students often feel it is necessary to negate the universal quantifier when taking the contrapositive. Don't fall into this trap!

1. The contrapositive of the stated theorem is

$$(\forall n \in \mathbb{Z})(n \text{ is odd} \Rightarrow n^2 \text{ is odd})$$

2. To prove this, let us assume that n is an odd integer.

3. Then by definition of odd, $(\exists k \in \mathbb{Z})$ such that $n = 2k + 1$.

4. Then by squaring

$$n^2 = (2k + 1)^2 = 4k^2 + 4k + 1 = 2(2k^2 + 2k) + 1$$

5. Let $q = 2k^2 + 2k$. By substitution, $n^2 = 2q + 1$.

6. Since the integers are closed under multiplication and addition, and since $k \in \mathbb{Z}$, we conclude that $q \in \mathbb{Z}$.

7. Since $n^2 = 2q + 1$ where $q \in \mathbb{Z}$, we conclude that n^2 is odd, so by the definition of an odd integer.

8. So we have proven that $(n \text{ odd}) \Rightarrow (n^2 \text{ odd})$.

9. Taking the contrapositive of this we get $(n^2 \text{ even}) \Rightarrow (n \text{ even})$ as required.

$\square$

Exercises

In exercises 1 through 7, write the contrapositive.

1. If n is even then n is divisible by 2.

2. If $p + q$ is even then either both are even or both are odd.

3. If $xy > 100$ then either $x > 10$ or $y > 10$

4. If n is prime then n is odd.

5. If n is an integer then $5n + 3$ is not divisible by 5.

6. If $\neg(7|n^2)$ then $\neg(7|n)$.

7. If n^2 is an odd integer then n is an odd integer.

8. Prove each of the statements in exercises 1 through 7 using the method of contraposition.

9 . Proof by Contradiction

Any proof by contraposition can be also rearranged to be a proof by contradiction. To see this suppose that we want to prove that $P \Rightarrow Q$ by contraposition. This means proving $\neq Q \Rightarrow \neg P$. The proof looks something like:

Proof. (Outline of Pseudo-Proof by Contraposition.)

1. Assume $\neg Q$.
2. Derive a consequence of $\neq Q$.
3. Derive a consequence of steps 1 and 2.
   ⋮ etc.

   n. Derive $\neg P$ as a consequences of steps 1 through n-1.
   n+1. $\therefore \neq Q \Rightarrow \neq P$
   n+2. $\therefore P \Rightarrow Q$ by contraposition of step n+1

   □

Here is a what proof by contradiction of the same statment would look like.

Proof. (Outline of Pseudo-poof by Contradiction.)

1. Suppose $\exists x$ such that $\neg(P(x) \Rightarrow Q(x))$, or equivalently, suppose that $\exists x$ such that $(P(x) \wedge \neg Q(x))$

2. Derive a consequence of step 1.

3. Derive a consequences of steps 1 and 2.

   ⋮ etc.

   n. Conclude $\neg P(x)$.

n+1. Observe that $\neg P(x)$ contradicts $P(x)$. Thus x satisfies both $P(x)$ and $\neg P(x)$, as well as $\neg Q(x)$.

n+2 Conclude no such x exists as a result of the contradition.

☐

▶ ▶ ▶ **Example 9.1.** We proved theorem 8.4 using contraposition. We repeat the proof using contradiction.

Proof. The statement to be proven is $(n^2$ even$) \Rightarrow (n$ even$)$.

This is equivalent to $\neg(n^2$ even$) \vee (n$ even $)$.

The negation of this is $\neg(\neg(n^2$ even$) \vee (n$ even $)) \equiv (n^2$ even $\wedge n$ odd$)$.

So: to prove by contradiction, assume that $(n^2$ even $\wedge n$ odd$)$.

Since n is odd, there is some integer k such that $n = 2k + 1$. Squaring,

$$n^2 = (2k+1)^2 = 4k^2 + 4k + 1 = 2(2k^2 + 2k) + 1$$

Let $q = 2k^2 + 2k$. Since the integers are closed under multiplication and addition, q is an integer. Hence $n^2 = 2k + 1$. This means that n^2 is odd.

This contradicts the fact that n^2 is even. Hence our assumption that $(n^2$ even $\wedge n$ odd$)$ must be **False**. This assumption was the negation of $(n^2$ even$) \Rightarrow (n$ even$)$, which must therefore be **True**. ☐

◀ ◀ ◀

Theorem 9.1.

$\sqrt{2}$ is irrational.

Proof. Prove by contradiction. Suppose that the $\sqrt{2}$ is rational.

Then ∃ integers m, n with no common factors such that $\sqrt{2} = m/n$. If necessary, divide out all common factors to obtain m and n.

Squaring gives $2 = m^2/n^2$.

Multiplying across by n^2, we obtain $m^2 = 2n^2$.

Thus m^2 is even (it is twice an integer). By theorem 8.4, m must also be even. Hence there exists some integer k such that $m = 2k$

Therefore by substitution,

$$2n^2 = m^2 = (2k)^2 = 4k^2$$

Dividing by 2, $n^2 = 2k^2$. Thus n^2 is even, and so n is also even.

Since n and m are both even, they are both divisible by 2. But by assumptions, n and m share no common factors.

This is a contradiction, so no such integer n and m can exists such that $\sqrt{2} = m/n$. Therefore $\sqrt{2}$ is irrational. $\square$

▶ ▶ ▶ **Example 9.2.** Use contradiction to prove that $1 + 3\sqrt{2}$ is irrational.

Proof. Suppose that $1 + 3\sqrt{2}$ is rational. Then $\exists a, b \in \mathbb{Z}$, with $b \neq 0$, such that

$$1 + 3\sqrt{2} = \frac{a}{b} \qquad \text{definition of rational}$$

$$3\sqrt{2} = \frac{a}{b} - 1 \qquad \text{subtract 1}$$

$$= \frac{a}{b} - \frac{b}{b} \qquad \text{substitute } 1 = \frac{b}{b}$$

$$= \frac{a - b}{b} \qquad \text{combine over common fraction}$$

$$\sqrt{2} = \frac{a - b}{3b} \qquad \text{divide by 3}$$

$$= \frac{\text{integer}}{\text{nonzero integer}}$$

which implies that $\sqrt{2} \in \mathbb{Q}$, which is a contradiction of the previous theorem.

Hence $1 + 3\sqrt{2}$ is irrational. $\square$

Definition 9.1. Divisibility

Let p and q be integers. We say that p **is divisible by** q, or alternatively, q **divides** p if there exists an integer k such that $p = kq$. We write $q|p$.

The expression q **divides** p can be thought of as a short form of saying q **divides into** p **without remainder**, or equivalently, q **is a factor of** p.

Theorem 9.2.

Suppose $a \in \mathbb{Z}$ and p is any prime factor of a. Then p is not a factor of $a + 1$.

Proof. (Proof by contradiction.)

Suppose that $\exists a \in \mathbb{Z}$ and a prime number p such that both $p|a$ and $p|(a + 1)$.

By the definition of divisibility, from the first condition $\exists r \in \mathbb{Z}$ such that $a = pr$, and from the second condition, $\exists s \in \mathbb{Z}$ such that $a + 1 = ps$.

Thus by substitution

$$1 = a + 1 - a = ps - pr = p(s - r) = pk$$

where $k = s - r$. Since $\mathbb{Z}$ is closed under subtraction, $k \in \mathbb{Z}$. But the equation $pk = 1$ tells us that $p|1$, i.e., p is a factor of 1.

We know that p is nether 1 nor -1 because p is prime. Since the only factors of 1 are 1 and -1, this is a contradition.

Thus the original assumption was **False**, and its negation is true. We conclude that p cannot be a factor of both a and $a + 1$. $\square$

Theorem 9.3.

The set of primes is infinite.

Proof. The proof is by contradiction. Suppose (by contradiction) that the set of primes is finite.

Then there must be some largest prime p.

We can then (in theory) list all the prime numbers in ascending order:

$$2, 3, 5, 7, 11, \ldots, p$$

Let N be the product of all of these primes.

$$N = 2 \cdot 3 \cdot 5 \cdot 7 \cdots p$$

Then $N > 1$, and hence $N + 1 > N > p$. Hence $N + 1$ is not prime itself, because p is the largest prime. Hence $N + 1$ is divisible by some prime number q, so that $q | (N + 1)$.

The set $S = \{2, 3, 5, 7, \ldots, p\}$ contains all the prime numbers, because we have assumed that there is a largest prime, so $q \in S$. Hence $q | N$. But by theorem 9.2, $\neg(q | (N + 1))$, which contradicts our earlier conclusion that $q | (N + 1)$.

Thus we have made a **False** assumption. The only assumption that we have made, however, is that there is a largest prime. Thus there must not be a largest prime. $\square$

▶ ▶ ▶ **Example 9.3.** Prove that $(\forall x \in \mathbb{Z}) \neg (9 | (x^2 - 3))$

Proof. Prove by contradiction. Suppose that $\exists x \in \mathbb{Z}$ such that $9 | (x^2 - 3)$

By definition of divisibility, $\exists q \in \mathbb{Z}$ such that

$$
\begin{aligned}
x^2 - 3 &= 9q && \text{def. of divisibility} \\
x^2 &= 3 + 9q && \text{add 3 to both sides} \\
&= 3(1 + 3q) && \text{factor 3 out of right side}
\end{aligned}
$$

From the prime factorization theorem we know that

$$x^2 = (p_1^{e_1} p_2^{e_2} \cdots p_n^{e_n})^2 = p_1^{2e_1} p_2^{2e_2} \cdots p_n^{2e_n}$$

for some prime numbers $p_1, \ldots, p_n$ and integers $e_1, \ldots, e_n$. Thus the exponent of each prime factor of x^2 is even.

In $x^2 = 3(1 + 3q)$ the exponent of 3, which is prime, is one, which is not even. Thus the prime factorization of $1 + 3q$ must contain an 3 raised to an odd power. Hence

$$3|(1 + 3q)$$

By the definition of divisibility, $\exists n \in \mathbb{Z}$ such that

$$
\begin{aligned}
1 + 3q &= 3n &&\text{def. of divisibility} \\
1 &= 3n - 3q &&\text{subtract 3q from both sides} \\
&= 3(n - q) &&\text{factor 3 out of right side} \\
n - q &= \frac{1}{3} &&\text{divide by 3}
\end{aligned}
$$

Since the $\mathbb{Z}$ is closed under subtraction, $n - q \in \mathbb{Z}$. Hence by the last setp, $1/3 \in \mathbb{Z}$. This contraditions the fact that $1/3 \notin \mathbb{Z}$. Hence our assumption "Suppose that $\exists x \in \mathbb{Z}$ such that $9|(x^2 - 3)$" must be False. Therefore $(\forall x \in \mathbb{Z}) \neg (9|(x^2 - 3))$. $\square$

◀ ◀ ◀

▶ ▶ ▶ **Example 9.4.** Prove that there is at most one real number b such that $(\forall x \in \mathbb{R})(bx = x)$.

Proof. We know that at least one such b exists, namely $b = 1$. This is because $1 \cdot x = x$ for all $x \in \mathbb{R}$.

To prove the proposition we need to show that no other $b \neq 1$ exists such that $b \cdot x = x$ for all x in $\mathbb{R}$.

Prove by contradiction: suppose that some other $b' \neq 1$ exists, where $b' \neq b$, also satisfies $b'x = x$ for all x in $\mathbb{R}$. Then

$$
\begin{aligned}
b'x &= x &&\text{assumption} \\
1x &= x &&\text{properties of } \mathbb{R} \\
b'x - 1x &= 0 &&\text{subtract the last two lines} \\
(b' - 1)x &= 0 &&\text{factor out an } x
\end{aligned}
$$

But for any two real numbers $x, y \in \mathbb{R}$, $xy = 0 \Rightarrow ((x = 0) \vee (y = 0))$.

Hence either $b' - 1 = 0$ or $x = 0$. Since $(b' - 1)x = 0$ for all $x \in \mathbb{R}$, the equation must hold both for $x = 0$ and $x \neq 0$. Hence $b' - 1 = 0$ or $b' = 1$.

Thus $b' = 1 = b$ which contradicts the assumption $b' \neq b$. Hence there is at most one real number b that satisfies the equation $bx = x$ for all $x \in \mathbb{R}$. $\square$

The **unique factorization theorem**, which is sometimes called the **fundamental theorem of arithmetic**, states that every positive integer has a unique prime factorization.

Theorem 9.4. Unique Factorization Theorem

Let n be a positive integer. Then there exist distinct prime numbers $p_1 \neq p_2 \neq \cdots \mid p_k$ and positive integers (sometimes called multiplicities) $\epsilon_1, \epsilon_2, \ldots, \epsilon_k$ such that

$$n = p_1^{\epsilon_1} p_2^{\epsilon_2} \cdots p_k^{\epsilon_k} = \prod_{j=1}^{k} p_j^{\epsilon_j}$$

such that any other factorization is identical except possibly for a reordering of the sequence of prime numbers.

Proof.

The existence part of the proof is given in the proof of theorem 10.1.

We will prove uniqueness by contradiction.

1. By theorem 10.1, one factorization already exists:

$$n = \prod_{j=1}^{k} p_j^{\epsilon_j}$$

2. Suppose that there is a different factorization,

$$n = \prod_{j=1}^{k} p_j^{\eta_j}$$

for some set of positive integers $\eta_1, \eta_2, \ldots, \eta_k$ with at least one of the $\eta_j \neq \epsilon_j$.

---

3. Then if both factorizations must be equal to one another,

$$\prod_{j=1}^{k} p_j^{\epsilon_j} = \prod_{j=1}^{k} p_j^{\eta_j}$$

4. Since at least one of the $\eta_j \neq \epsilon_j$, let it be at some index q. Then

$$p_q^{\epsilon_q} \prod_{j \neq q}^{k} p_j^{\epsilon_j} = p_q^{\eta_q} \prod_{j \neq q}^{k} p_j^{\eta_j}$$

5. Because $\eta_q \neq \epsilon_q$, either $\eta_q > \epsilon_q$ or $\eta_q < \epsilon_q$.
6. Suppose the first inequality holds (it does not matter which one holds, the proof is identical with the variables reversed). Then divide both sides by $p_q^{\epsilon_q}$

$$\prod_{j \neq q}^{k} p_j^{\epsilon_j} = (p_q^{\eta_q}/p_q^{\epsilon_q}) \prod_{j \neq q}^{k} p_j^{\eta_j} = p_q^{\eta_q - \epsilon_q} \prod_{j \neq q}^{k} p_j^{\eta_j}$$

7. Then p_q is not a factor on the left, but it is a factor on the right with multiplicity $\eta_q - \epsilon_q > 0$.
8. This is a contradiction, because the left hand side and right hand side of the equation are the same integer. So if p divides into one side, it must divide into the other side.
9. So our assumption that there was a different factorization was false.

Hence the prime factorization is unique. $\quad \square$

Exercises

1. Show that $\sqrt{2}/2$ is irrational.

2. Show that the square root of an irrational number is irrational.

3. Show that $\sqrt{5}$ is irrational.

4. Show that $1 + 3\sqrt{5}$ is irrational.

5. Show that $\sqrt{2} + \sqrt{5}$ is irrational.

6. Is the sum of two irrational numbers always irrational?

7. Is the product of two irrational numbers always irrational?

10 . Induction

Mathematical induction shows that a property is true for all positive integers, one step at a time. It is analogous to a the very commonly used programming tool of recursion, and we will see that the two (induction and recursion) have a lot in common.

In its most common form, induction starts at $n = 1$, but it can start at any integer (generalized induction). Induction is used to recursively prove that a property is true for all integers greater than or equal to a base value (where the base value is traditionally one).

Mathematically, induction is closely related to the **Well Ordering Principle**. The well ordering principle states that every non-empty set of non-negative integers has a least element. For computational scientists, mathematical induction, and its generalization to data structures, **structural induction**, are far more useful than the well ordering principle, which is of mostly theoretical interest. The well ordering principle remains useful mostly for proving theoretical results such as the quotient-remainder theorem (theorem 11.1).

Definition 10.1. Principle of Mathematical Induction

To prove that a statement $P(n)$ is true $\forall n \in \mathbb{Z}^+$:
  1. Prove $P(1)$ (This is called the **basis step**.)
  2. Assume $P(k)$ is true. (This is called the **inductive hypothesis**.)
  3. Prove $P(k) \Rightarrow P(k + 1)$ (This is called the **inductive step**.)

▶ ▶ ▶ **Example 10.1.** Use induction to prove that $\displaystyle\sum_{k=1}^{n} k = \frac{n(n + 1)}{2}$.

Proof. Basis Step. For $n = 1$,

$$\sum_{k=1}^{1} k = 1 = \frac{1(1 + 1)}{2}$$

<u>Inductive Hypothesis.</u> Assume that $\displaystyle\sum_{k=1}^{n} k = \frac{n(n+1)}{2}$.

<u>Inductive Step.</u> We need to show that $\displaystyle\sum_{k=1}^{n+1} k = \frac{(n+1)(n+2)}{2}$. (Substitute $n+1$ for n into both sides of the equation.) But

$$\sum_{k=1}^{n+1} k = \left(\sum_{k=1}^{n} k \right) + (n+1)$$

$$= \frac{n(n+1)}{2} + (n+1) \qquad\qquad \text{by inductive hypothesis}$$

$$= \frac{n(n+1) + 2(n+1)}{2} \qquad\qquad \text{common denominator}$$

$$= \frac{(n+2)(n+1)}{2} \qquad\qquad \text{distributive law; result as required.}$$

$\square$

◀ ◀ ◀

Sometimes we modify the principle of mathematical induction as follows.

Definition 10.2. Principle of Mathematical Induction (generalized)

To prove that a statement $P(n)$ is true $(\forall n \geqslant m)(n \in \mathbb{Z}^{+})$:
1. Prove $P(m)$ (This is called the **basis step**.)
2. Assume $P(k)$ is true (where $k > m$). (The **inductive hypothesis**.)
3. Prove $P(k) \Rightarrow P(k+1)$ (This is called the **inductive step**.)

▶ ▶ ▶ **Example 10.2.** Prove that $2^n < n!$ for all $n \geqslant 4$.

Proof. <u>Basis Step.</u> For $n = 4$,

$$2^4 = 16 < 24 = 4!$$

<u>Inductive Hypothesis.</u> Let $n \geqslant 4$ and assume that $2^n < n!$.

<u>Inductive Step.</u> We need to show that $2^{n+1} < (n+1)!$. But

$$2^{n+1} = 2^n \cdot 2 \qquad\qquad \text{definition of } 2^{n+1}$$

$$< 2n! \qquad \text{using inductive hypothesis}$$
$$< (n+1)n! \qquad \text{because } 2 < 4 < n+1$$
$$= (n+1)! \qquad \text{This is the desired result}$$

□

◀ ◀ ◀

A third version of the principle is called **Strong Induction**

Definition 10.3. Principle of Mathematical Induction (strong)

To prove that a statement $P(n)$ is true ($\forall n \geqslant a \in \mathbb{Z}^+$):
1. Prove $P(a), P(a+1), \ldots, P(n)$ are true (where $a, a+1, \ldots, n$ are integers). (**basis step**)
2. Assume $P(a), P(a+1), \ldots, P(n)$ are true. (**inductive hypothesis**)
3. Prove $P(a) \wedge P(a+1) \wedge \cdots \wedge P(n) \Rightarrow P(n+1)$ (**inductive step.**)

In definition 3, **if any of $P(a), P(a+1), \ldots, P(n)$ are false than the proof by strong induction is invalid**. So it is not sufficient to merely say that $P(1)$ is true and then jump to the assumption that $P(1), P(2), \ldots, P(n)$ are all true. You can only make valid assumptions. The following is a bad proof by strong induction that is given in many textbooks of how not to use strong induction.

▶ ▶ ▶ **Example 10.3.** A Bad Proof Using Strong Induction. Prove that $a^n = 1$ for all $n \in \mathbb{N}$ and for all $a \neq 0$.

Proof. Basis Step. Since $a \neq 0$, $a^0 = 1$ by definition of the zeroth power.

Inductive Hypothesis. Assume $a^n = 1$ for all integers $n = 0, 1, \ldots, k$. We need to show that $a^{k+1} = 1$.

Inductive Step.

$$a^{k+1} = \frac{a^k \cdot a^k}{a^{k-1}} \qquad \text{Properties of Exponents}$$
$$= \frac{1 \cdot 1}{1} \qquad \text{Inductive Hypothesis}$$
$$= 1 \qquad \text{Required result.}$$

Can you identify the error(s)?　　　◀ ◀ ◀

▶ ▶ ▶ **Example 10.4.** Define the sequence $b_1, b_2, b_3, \ldots$ as follows:

$$b_1 = 3, \ b_2 = 6, \ b_k = b_{k-1} + b_{k-2} \ k = 3, 4, \ldots$$

Prove that 3 is a factor b_k for all $k \in \mathbb{Z}^+$.

> *Proof.* Basis Step. Since 3 is a factor of both 3 and 6, the conjecture holds for both $k = 1$ and $k = 2$.
>
> Inductive Hypothesis. Suppose that b_k is divisible by 3 for all values of $k = 1, 2, \ldots, n - 1$.
>
> Inductive Step. By the inductive hypothesis, there exist integers $p_1, p_2, \ldots, p_{n-1}$ such that
>
> $$b_1 = 3p_1, b_2 = 3p_2, \ldots, b_{m-2} = 3p_{m-2}, b_{m-1} = 3p_{m-1}$$
>
> Thus by the definition of the sequence
>
> $$\begin{aligned} b_m &= b_{m-1} + b_{m-2} \\ &= 3p_{m-1} + 3p_{m-2} && \text{substitution} \\ &= 3(p_{m-1} + p_{m-2}) && \text{distributive property} \end{aligned}$$
>
> Since $p_{m-1} + p_{m-2}$ is an integer, we conclude that 3 is a factor of b_m, as required. □

◀ ◀ ◀

Note that if we had only said "the conjecture holds for $k = 1$" in the basis step and left the rest of the proof unchanged this would have been insufficient. Suppose, for example, that we had been given, instead, $b_1 = 3$ and $b_2 = 7$. Then the subsequent inductive hypothesis would have been false.

Strong induction can be used to prove the existence of a prime factorizpation for every integer, as shown in theorem 10.1. Usually this is written as

$$n = \prod p_i^{\epsilon_i} = p_1^{\epsilon_1} p_2^{\epsilon_2} \cdots$$

where $p_1, p_2, \ldots$ are distinct (different) prime numbers and each ϵ_i is a positive integer. In theorem 10.1 the f_i are not necessarily all distinct, so we do not specify the exponents.

> ### Theorem 10.1. Prime Factorization Theorem (Existence)
>
> Every integer $n \geqslant 2$ can be decomposed into a product of prime factors, i.e., for every integer $n \geqslant 2$, there exist prime numbers $f_1, f_2, \ldots f_k$ such that $n = f_1 f_2 \ldots f_k$.

Proof. <u>Basis Step.</u> Since 2 is prime, the statement is true for $n = 2$.

<u>Inductive Hypothesis.</u> Suppose that each integer $2, 3, \ldots, n$ can be decomposed into a product of prime factors.

<u>Inductive Step.</u> We need to show that $n + 1$ can be decomposed into a product of prime factors.

Either $n + 1$ is prime (case 1) or it is not prime (case 2).

Case 1: If $n + 1$ is prime, then $n + 1$ is already decomposed into a product of prime factors, and the desired result is true.

Case 2: Suppose $n + 1$ is not prime.

1. Since $n + 1$ is not prime, it has at two positive factors p and q, such that $2 < p < n + 1$ and $2 < q < n + 1$, and $n + 1 = pq$.
2. By the inductive hypothesis, each of the numbers p and q can be decomposed into a product of primes.
3. Thus $n + 1 = pq = $ (product of primes) $\times$ (product of primes) as required.

$\square$

Factorization in Python

By taking advantage of the fact that the only even prime is 2, we can easily double the speed of a brute-force factorization algorithm, as illustrated in the following code. The function **prime_factorization(n)** returns a list of the prime factors in standard form. The factors are accrued in the variable **factors** which is returned as the value of the function. The first **while** loop returns all the instances of 2 in the factorization. Then the **for** loop considers each subsequently larger possible factor. Within the inner **while**, each instance of these factors will subsequently be appended to the list **factors**. Composite numbers will not be added to the list, because when subsequent composite numbers by the **for** loop, such as 9, are reached, the test **n%i==0** will always fail, because all factors of the composite number will have already been found, and so the composite factors will be omitted from the list. Finally, there could posibly be a single prime factor that is greater than $\sqrt{n}$, as with $333 = 3 \times 3 \times 37$. If this is the case, the value of n will be left equal to this factor at the end of the second loop, and it will be caught on the way out by the final **if** statement.

```python
from math import sqrt
def prime_factorization(n):
    # verify that the input is an integer > 2
    if not isinstance(n,int): return([])
    if n<2: return([])

    factors=[]
    while n % 2 == 0:          # remove factors of 2
        factors.append(2)
        n = n // 2

    for i in range(3,int(sqrt(n))+1,2): # odd factors
        while n % i==0:
            factors.append(i)
            n = n // i

    if n > 2:
        factors.append(n)
    return factors
```

To see how it works, we try the following factorizations:

```python
print (prime_factorization(123456789))
print (prime_factorization(333))
print (prime_factorization(360))
```

```
[3, 3, 3607, 3803]
[3, 3, 37]
[2, 2, 2, 3, 3, 5]
```

Exercises

1. Suppose that $a_1 = 5$, $a_2 = 10$, and $a_k = a_{k-1} + a_{k-2}$ for $k = 3, 4, \ldots$. Use strong induction to prove that 5 is factor of a_n for all $n \geqslant 3$.

2. Use induction to prove that the sum of all the odd integers 1, 3, 5, 7, $\ldots, n$ to any odd integer n is a perfect square.

3. Prove using induction that

$$\sum_{k=1}^{n} k^2 = \frac{n(n+1)(2n+1)}{6}$$

4. Prove using induction that

$$\sum_{k=1}^{n} k^3 = \frac{n^2(n+1)^2}{4}$$

5. Prove that the sum of a geometric seris is

$$\sum_{k=0}^{n-1} ar^k = \frac{a - ar^n}{1 - r}$$

where $|r| < 1$.

6. The following code was suggested by a user on Stack Overflow as a possible (but very inefficient) way to implement a recurse prime factorization.

```
def primeFact (i, f):
    if i < f:
        return []
    if i % f == 0:
        return [f] + primeFact (i / f, 2)
    return primeFact (i, f + 1)
```

To invoke this code you would type **primeFact (n,2)**, e.g., to get the prime factors of 28 you would type **primeFact (28,2)**. Can you come up with a more efficient recursive code to calculate the prime factorization, e.g., one that would not have to go though every single integer? For example, the code in the text skips all of the even numbers after 2 and stops at $\sqrt{n}$.

11. Division

If an integer d is a factor of n then we said earlier that $d|n$ (def. defdef-divisibility). If it is not a factor, then d will divide into n and non-integral number of times and have a remainder.

Theorem 11.1. Quotient-Remainder Theorem

For every integer n and for every positve integer d, there exist unique integers q and r such that
$$n = dq + r$$
where $0 \leqslant r < d$. Then q is **quotient** of the fraction n/d with **numerator** n, **denominator** d, and **remainder** r.

Proof. The theorem states both the existence and the uniqueness of integers q (the quotient) and r (the remainder) in the expression $n = dq + r$, so we have two things to prove.

Existence.

1. Let n and d be given.
2. Define the set $S = \{x \in \mathbb{N} | x = n - dk, \ \forall k \in \mathbb{Z}\}$
3. If $n \geqslant 0$, then $n - 0d = n \geqslant 0$ hence $n \in S$.
4. If $n < 0$ then $n - n \cdot d = n(1 - d)$ is the product of a negative number (n) and a non-postive number (since $d \geqslant 1$). Hence $n - n \cdot d \geqslant 0 \in S$.
5. By steps 3 and 4, S is non empty - it has at least one element.
6. By the well-ordering principle S has a smallest element. Call this smallest element r.
7. Since every element in S can be written in the form $x = n - dk$ then there exists a $k = q$ such that $r = n - dq$ for some q (we have not yet fixed the value of q).
8. Solving for n gives $n = dq + r$.

This proves that some q, r exist. Next, we show that $r < d$ by contradiction.

1. Suppose $r \geqslant d$
2. Then $n - d(q+1) = d - dq - d = r - d \geqslant 0$
3. Thus $n - d(q+1) < r$
4. But $n - d(q+1) \in S$ by defnition of S
5. Since r is the smallest item in S, we have a contradiction with $n - d(q+1)$ being a smaller iterm than r that is also in S.
6. Hence our only assumption, that $r \geqslant d$, is incorrect.

Thus there exist integers q and r such that $0 \leqslant r < d$ as required.

Uniqueness.

1. Let r, q be a remainder and quotient with $0 \leqslant r < d$ such that $n = dq + r$.
2. Let r', q' be a second remainder and quotient with $0 \leqslant r' < d$, such that $n = dq' + r'$.
3. Equating the two expressions for n gives $dq + r = dq' + r'$.
4. Rerranging, $r - r' = d(q' - q)$.
5. Thus $d | (r - r')$
6. Hence $|d| < |r - r'|$
7. From steps 1 and 2, $0 \leqslant r < |d|$ and $-|d| < -r' \leqslant 0$.
8. Adding the inequalities gives $-|d| < r - r' < |d|$
9. Thus $|r - r'| < d$, shich contradicts with step 6.
10. Thus our assumption that there was a second set r', q' is false.

Therefore the quotient q and remainder r are unique. $\square$

We define the **div** and **mod** operations based on the results of integer division as defined in this manner. In Python 3, **div** between integers is obtained with the double slash (as in **17//3**, which should return **5**). Only using a single slash will revert to floating point division (**17/3** gives **5.66667**). The **mod** operation is given by the percent sign (as in **17%3**, which returns **2**).

Definition 11.1. div and mod

We define n **div** d as the integer quotient, and n **mod** d as the integer remainder r when n is divided by a nonzero integer d.

$$n = dq + r = d(n \textbf{ div } d) + (n \textbf{ mod } d)$$

Ch. 11. Division

Definition 11.2. Greatest Common Divisor (GCD)

Let a and b be integers that are not both zero. Their **greatest common divisor**, denoted by $\gcd(a, b)$ is the integer d with the following properties:

1. d is a common divisor: $d|a$ and $d|b$

2. If c is any other common divisor of a and b then $c \leqslant d$.

The following theorem leads to a constructive algorithm for determining the gcd.

Theorem 11.2. Reduction of gcd

If a and b are any integers that are not both zero, and if q and r are integers such that $a = bq + r$ then

$$\gcd(a, b) = \gcd(b, r)$$

Proof. We will prove the theorem in two steps. First we will prove that $\gcd(a, b) \leqslant \gcd(b, r)$. Then we will prove that $\gcd(a, b) \geqslant \gcd b, r$. The consequence is that both must be equal.

Proof that $\gcd(a, b) \leqslant \gcd(b, r)$.

1. let a, b be integers, not both zero, and let p and q be integers such that $a = bq + r$ (Hypothesis of the theorem).
2. Let c be an integer such that $c|a$ and $c|b$.
3. Hence there exists some integers m and n such that $a = nc$ and $b = nc$ (definition of divisbility).
4. By substitution, $nc = a = bq + r = mcq + r$ (using the fact that $a = bq + r$, as given in step 1).
5. Solving for r gives $r = nc - mcq = c(n - mq)$.
6. Since $n - mq \in \mathbb{Z}$ (by the closure of the integer), $c|r$.
7. Thus every common divisor of a and b is also a common divisor of both b and r.
8. Let $z = \gcd(a, b)$. Then $z|b$ and by the previous step, $z|r$.
9. Since z is a divsor of both b and r, it is no larger than the

greatest common divisor of b and r: $z \leqslant \gcd(b, r)$
10. Combining the last two steps, $\gcd(a, b) \leqslant \gcd(b, r)$.

Proof that $\gcd(a, b) \geqslant \gcd(b, r)$.

This part of the proof is completely analogous to the first part of the proof, and is left as an exercise.

Since both $\gcd(a, b) \leqslant \gcd(b, r)$ and $\gcd(a, b) \geqslant \gcd b, r$ the only possibility is that $\gcd(a, b) = \gcd(b, r)$. □

Euclidean Algorithm The previous theorem provides the basis for the **Euclidean Algorithm** for finding the greatest common divisor:

1. Let A and B be positive integers such that $A > B$.

2. If $B = 0$ then return A and the algorithm is done.

3. If $B \neq 0$ then $B > 0$. By the quotient-remainder theorem (theorem 11.1), there are some numbers r, q, such that $A = Bq + r$, where $0 \leqslant r < B$. So find r.

4. Replace the original prolem (Find $\gcd(A, B)$) with the modified problem: Find $\gcd(B, r)$ (as justified by theorem 11.2).

5. Repeat the process, starting from step 1, but with A, B replaced by B, r

▶ ▶ ▶ **Example 11.1.** Find gcd(330,156).

1. $330 = 2 \cdot 156 + 18$
2. Replace gcd(330, 156) with gcd(156, 18)
3. $156 = 8 \cdot 18 + 12$
4. Replace gcd(156, 18) with gcd(18,12)
5. $18 = 1 \cdot 12 + 6$
6. Replace gcd(18, 12) with gcd(12, 6)
7. $12 = 2 \cdot 6 + 0$
8. Replace gcd(12, 6) with gcd(6,0)
9. The gcd is 6

◀ ◀ ◀

The Euclidean algorithmm is easily implemented in Python. The following illustrates the calculation of gcd(12345,333)=3.

```
x=12345
y=333
while y>0:
    x,y=y,x%y
    print(x,y)
print(x)
```

333 24
24 21
21 3
3 0
3

Exercises

1. Complete the missing steps in the proof of theorem 11.2.

2. Find values of q and r that solve $n = dq + r$ for each of the following combindations of values of n and d.

   a) $n = 10, d = 3$
   b) $n = 37, d = 5$
   c) $n = 25, d = 4$
   d) $n = 16, d = 8$

3. An easier way to compute the gcd in python is to use the function **gcd** in the **math** library. Using **math.gcd**, calculate the following gcds:

   a) gcd(12345,333)
   b) gcd(2440,360)
   c) gcd(2441, 360)

4. Repeat the calculation of the above gcds using the Euclidean algorithm.

12 . Functions

A **function** is a rule that matches items in one set with items in another set. If we call the first set S and the second set T we say the function maps the set S to the set T and write $f : S \mapsto T$. It is possible that not every item in T will have an item mapped to it, and it is also possible that not every item in S will map to an item in T. The collection of items in S that map to items in T are call the **domain** of the function. The collection of items in T that have items that are mapped to them are called the **range** of the function. The set T is called the **codomain of the function**. If $s \in S$ is mapped to $t \in T$ by the function then we write $t = f(s)$.

Consider the following mapping. Let

$$S = \{A, B, C, D\}$$
$$T = \{\alpha, \beta, \gamma, \delta\}$$

Define the function $f : S \mapsto T$ by

$$f(A) = \alpha; f(B) = \beta; f(C) = \delta; f(D) = \delta$$

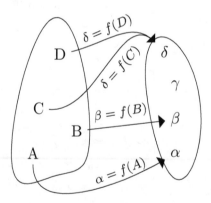

The the domain of f is $\{A, B, C, D\}$; the codomain of f is $\{\alpha, \beta, \gamma, \delta\}$; and the range of f is $\{\alpha, \beta, \delta\}$.

For example, suppose an auto dealer maintains an inventory of all the vehicles in its stock. Within the database there is a function **door-tint** that tells whether the window tint is **clear**, **lightgrey**, **dark**, **privacy**, **top-25-percent-dark**. Depending on the current inventory in stock, there may be more than car available that is mapped to each one of these categories, or there may be some categories for which there are no vehicles currently available. If the dealarship stocks motorcycles, for example, they would not be mapped to anything.

When we look at functions, we are generally interested in two very important questions.

- Is the function one-to-one?

  A function is one-to-one if no two values in the domain are mapped to the same value.

- Is the function onto?

  A function is onto if it is mapped to every value in the range.

Definition 12.1. One to One

We say that a function is **one-to-one** (or injective) if

$$f(a) = f(b) \Rightarrow a = b$$

for all a and b in the domain.

▶ ▶ ▶ **Example 12.1.** The function $y = x^2$ is not one-to-one on the domain Z because both -1 and 1 are mapped to the same number. ◀ ◀ ◀

Definition 12.2. Onto

We say that function $f : A \mapsto B$ is **onto**, or **surjective**, if and only

$$(\forall b \in B)(\exists a \in A)(f(a) = b)$$

In discrete math we are often dealing with integer domains. This often confuses students because functions that they might have previously expected to be one-to-one or onto in the real numbers are neither in the integers.

▶ ▶ ▶ **Example 12.2.** The function $f : \mathbb{R}^+ \mapsto \mathbb{R}^+$ given by $y = x^2$ is onto because every positve real number has a positve square root. Thus for any $y > 0$, there is a number x such that $y = x^2$. ◀ ◀ ◀

▶ ▶ ▶ **Example 12.3.** The function $f : \mathbb{Z}^+ \mapsto \mathbb{Z}^+$ given by $y = x^2$ is not onto because there are many positve real integers that do not have positive square roots.

> *Proof.* Proof by contrdiction and counter-example.
>
> 1. Suppose that f is onto.
> 2. Then since 11 is an integer (for example), there exists a x such that $11 = y = x^2$, where x is an integer.
> 3. Hence $\sqrt{x}$ is an integer.
> 4. This is a contradiction, since we know that there is no integer equal to $\sqrt{11}$.
> 5. Thus our assumption is wrong. But we only made one assumption, which was that f is onto.
>
> Hence f is not onto. □

◀ ◀ ◀

Definition 12.3. One-to-One Correspondence

We say that a function is a **one-to-one-correspondence** if it is one-to-one and onto.

A one-to-one correspondence is sometimes called a **bijection**. If a function is bijective (is a bijection), then we can define an inverse function of $f :$ $A \mapsto B$, where $b = f(a)$, as the function that assigns to each element of B the unique element of A such that $f(a) = b$. We denote the inverse functoin by f^{-1}, so that if $b = f(a)$ then $a = f^{-1}(b)$.

Theorem 12.1. Existence of Inverse Function

Suppose that $f : A \mapsto B$. Then f has an inverse if and only if f is a bijection.

Ch. 12. Functions

Convergence of Functions

We are interested in describing how fast functions grow in terms of some parameter. In particular, we will be interested in comparing the growth of these functions to a list of well-understood and known functions that can be catalogued. This information is particularly useful in theoretically predicting the efficiency of an algorithm by counting the number of steps (e.g., the number of multiplications, or comparisons, or program lines of code executed). We will see that many different types of algorithms can be grouped together into classes that are described by these canonical types of growth functions (e.g., logarithmic, linear, quadratic, exponentical, and so on).

Definition 12.4. Big-Oh Notation

We say $f(x) = O(g(x))$ if there are constants C and k such that

$$|f(x)| \leqslant C|g(x)|$$

for all $x > k$. We say that $f(x)$ is "big-oh" of $g(x)$.

We can use big-oh to give us an upper bound on the growth of a function; example 4 shows us a function that grows no faster (ultimately, in the sense of large enough x) than (a constant times) $g(x) = x^2$.

▶ ▶ ▶ **Example 12.4.** Let $f(x) = 5x^2 + 7x$. Then

$$|f(x)| \leqslant |5x^2| + |7x| \qquad \text{triangle inequality}$$
$$\leqslant |5x^2| + |7x^2| \qquad \text{because } x \leqslant x^2 \text{ for } x > 1$$
$$= 12|x^2| \qquad \text{addition}$$

Hence $f(x) = 5x^2 + 7x = O(x^2)$. ◀ ◀ ◀

Definition 12.5. Big-Omega Notation

We say $f(x) = \Omega(g(x))$ if there are constants C and k such that
$$|f(x)| \geqslant C|g(x)|$$
for all $x > k$. We say that $f(x)$ is "big-omega" of $g(x)$.

We can use big-oh to give an upper bound on the growth of a function, and big-omega to give a lower bound on the growth of a function. Ideally, we would like to bring these bounds as close together as possible. If we can find a function that is both big-oh and big-omega of $f(x)$, then we can provide a fairly tight bounds on how fast the function grows, in the sense that we can define what class of functions $f(x)$ is most similar to.

▶ ▶ ▶ **Example 12.5.** Let $f(x) = 5x^2 + 7x$. Then

$$|f(x)| = x^2|5 + 1.2/x| \qquad \text{factoring}$$
$$\geqslant 5x^2 \qquad \text{since } 1.2/x > 0 \text{ for } x \text{ large}$$

Hence $f(x) = 5x^2 + 7x = \Omega(x^2)$. ◀ ◀ ◀

Example 5 shows that $f(x) = x^2$ is $\Omega(x^2)$; we showed in example 4 that the same function was $O(x^2)$. So sometimes it is possible to find a function that both big-oh and big-omega of the same of function.

Definition 12.6. Big-Theta Notation

If there is a function $g(x)$ such that $f(x) = O(g(x))$ and $f(x) = \Omega(g(x))$, i.e., there are constants C_1, C_2 and k such that

$$C_1|g(x)| \leqslant |f(x)| \leqslant C_2|g(x)|$$

for all $x > k$. We say that $f(x)$ is "big-theta" of $g(x)$, and that $f(x)$ **has the same order** as $g(x)$ or **grows at the same order** as $g(x)$.

▶ ▶ ▶ **Example 12.6.** Examples 4 and 5 shows that $f(x) = 5x^2 + 7x = \Theta(x^2)$. ◀ ◀ ◀

▶ ▶ ▶ **Example 12.7.** The integral definition of the natural logarithm is given by

$$\ln x = \int_1^x \frac{1}{u} du$$

Fig. 12.1 illustrates that

$$\sum_{k=2}^{\lfloor x \rfloor} \frac{1}{k} < \ln x < \sum_{k=1}^{\lfloor x \rfloor} \frac{1}{k}$$

Figure 12.1.: The function $y = 1/x$ is bounded above and below by subsequences of the harmonic sequence $1/k$.

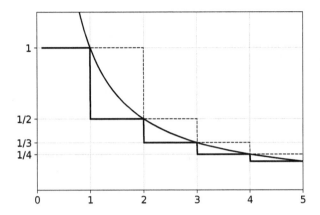

If we define the **finite harmonic series** $H(x)$ as

$$H(x) = \sum_{k=1}^{\lfloor x \rfloor} \frac{1}{k}$$

then we have

$$H(x) - 1 < \ln x < H(x)$$

The second inequality tells us that $H(x) = \Omega(\ln x)$ (multiplicative constant $= 1$). The first inequality gives us

$$H(x) < 1 + \ln x < \ln x + \ln x = 2 \ln x$$

for all $x > e$. Hence $H(x) = O(\ln x)$ with $C = 2$.

Since $H(x) = O(\ln x)$ and $H(x) = \Omega(\ln x)$ we may conclude that $H(x) = \Theta(\ln x)$. ◀ ◀ ◀

Exercises

1. Define each of the following:

   a) A function that maps from a set with 3 items to a set with 4 items

   b) A function that maps from a set with 4 items to a set with 3 items that is onto.

   c) A function that maps from a set with 4 items to a set with 3 items that is not onto.

   d) A function that maps from a set with 3 itmes to a set with 3 items that is not one to one.

2. Is is possible to define a function from a finite set to a smaller finite set that is one to one? If so, come up with an example. If not, prove it.

3. Is it possible to define a function from a finite set to a larger finite set that is onto? If so, come up with an example. If not, prove it.

4. Prove or disprove the following statement: If f is a bijection between two finite sets, does that mean that the sets must have the same size?

5. Find the smallest value of n such that $f(x)$ is $O(x^n)$ for each of the following.

   a) $3x^2 - 4x + 12$
   b) $x + x \ln x$
   c) $x + 10$
   d) $\ln x$
   e) $(x^2 + 2x + 1)/(x + 1)$
   f) $7x^5 + x \ln x$

6. Show that $n! = O(n^n)$.

7. Show that $2^n = O(n!)$ but that $n!$ is not $O(2^n)$.

13 . Sequences, Sums and Products

Mathematically, sequences are formalizations of functions on the integers. The are most frequently represented as a_n rather than $a(n)$ or $f(n)$. Usually their domain is the non-negative integers (although it is possible to define sequences on the positive integers, all integers, or any subset of the integers). The range of a sequence is most commonly the positive integers. A sequence defined on a finite subset of the integers is called a finite sequence. If the sequence has infinite extent, we often will express it with ellipse (dots), such as

$$a_0, a_1, a_2, \ldots$$

We will sometimes use a notation that is similar to set-builder notation, such as

$$a_k = \frac{k+2}{k+3}, k \geqslant = 0$$

which is equivalent to

$$a_0 = \frac{2}{3}, a_1 = \frac{3}{4}, a_2 = \frac{4}{5}, \ldots$$

or

$$\{a_k\}_{k \geqslant 0} = \{2/3, 3/4, 4/5, \ldots\}$$

and so forth. Sometimes we will just write out the numbers, as in

$$2/3, 3/4, 4/5, \ldots$$

If a sequence extends to both negative infinity (in index) as well as positive infinity, we might write

$$\ldots, a_{-2}, a_{-1}, a_0, a_1, a_2, \ldots$$

For example,

$$\ldots, 3^{-2}, 3^{-1}, 3^0, 3^1, 3^2, \ldots$$

is a sequence of all the integer powers of 3, where $a_k = 3^k$, and k is any integer.

▶ ▶ ▶ **Example 13.1.** Compute the first 5 terms of the sequence $a_k = k^2/(k^2 + 1)$, $k \geqslant 0$.

$$a_0 = 0^2/(0^2 + 1) = 0$$

$$a_1 = 1^1/(1^2 + 1) = 1/2$$
$$a_2 = 2^2/(2^2 + 1) = 4/5$$
$$a_3 = 3^2/(3^2 + 1) = 9/10$$
$$a_4 = 4^2/(4^2 + 1) = 16/17$$

Writing out the sequence,

$$0, 1/2, 4/5, 9/10, 16/17, \ldots$$

Definition 13.1. Alternating Sequence

An **alternating sequence** is a sequence that changes signs with each term.

▶ ▶ ▶ **Example 13.2.** Write out the first 5 terms of the alternating sequence $c_k = (-1)^k/2k, k \geqslant 1$

$$c_1 = (-1)^1/(2 \cdot 1) = -1/2$$
$$c_2 = (-1)^2/(2 \cdot 2) = 1/4$$
$$c_3 = (-1)^3/(2 \cdot 3) = -1/6$$
$$c_4 = (-1)^4/(2 \cdot 4) = 1/8$$
$$c_5 = (-1)^5/(2 \cdot 5) = -1/10$$

Writing out the first few terms of the series gives

$$-1/2, 1/4, -1/6, 1/8, -1/10, \cdots$$

Finding an explicit formula for a given sequence is sometimes a process of trial and error.

▶ ▶ ▶ **Example 13.3.** Find an explicit formula for the sequence

$$3, 6, 12, 24, 48, 96, \ldots$$

We observe that each term is twice its predecessor:

$$3, 2 \cdot 3, 2^2 \cdot 3, 2^3 \cdot 3, 2^4 \cdot 3, 2^5 \cdot 3, \ldots$$

so we might try $c_k = 3 \cdot 2^k, k = 0, 1, 2, \ldots$. To verify this we would have to plug in a few values of k and verify that it works. ◀ ◀ ◀

Ch. 13. Sequences, Sums and Products

A **series** is the sum of a sequence. We use the upper-case Greek letter sigma, $\sum$, to indicate a summation. We write this either as

$$\sum_{k=m}^{n} a_k = a_m + a_{m+1} + \cdots + a_{n-1} + a_n$$

or

$$\sum_{k=m}^{n} a_k = a_m + a_{m+1} + \cdots + a_{n-1} + a_n$$

The left hand side of the equation is read is as "The sum from (whatever is written on the bottom) to (whatever is written on the top) of (whatever is written next to the sigma)." When typeset, second form is typically used "in-line", as in $\sum_{k=1}^{10} a_k$, while the first form is typically used for equations that are set out in the middle of their own line (display equations).

▶ ▶ ▶ **Example 13.4.** Compute $\sum_{k=1}^{5} k^2$.

$$\sum_{k=1}^{5} k^2 = 1^2 + 2^2 + 3^2 + 4^2 + 5^2$$
$$= 1 + 4 + 9 + 16 + 25$$
$$= 55$$

◀ ◀ ◀

▶ ▶ ▶ **Example 13.5.** Write the sum of sequence $1/2, 1/2^2, 1/2^3, \ldots, 1/2^n$ using the big-sigma notation.

$$S = \sum_{k=1}^{n} \frac{1}{2^k}$$

◀ ◀ ◀

Definition 13.2. Series

An infinite series, denoted by $\sum_{k=0}^{\infty} a_k$, is the sum over all the terms in the infinite sequence a_k. The value of the sum S is determined by finding the limited of **partial sums**,

$$S = \sum_{k=0}^{\infty} a_k = \lim_{n \to \infty} \sum_{k=0}^{n} a_k$$

if the limit exists.

▶ ▶ ▶ **Example 13.6.** Find

$$S = \frac{1}{2 \cdot 3} + \frac{2}{3 \cdot 4} + \frac{3}{4 \cdot 5} + \frac{4}{5 \cdot 6} + \cdots + \frac{n}{(n+1)(n+2)}$$

for $n = 1$, $n = 2$, $n = 3$.

For $n = 1$,

$$S = \frac{1}{6}$$

For $n = 2$,

$$S = \frac{1}{6} + \frac{2}{12} = \frac{1}{3}$$

For $n = 3$,

$$S = \frac{1}{3} + \frac{3}{4 \cdot 5} = \frac{20}{60} + \frac{9}{60} = \frac{29}{60}$$

◀ ◀ ◀

One trick that we often find useful in analyzing series is that of separating off the last term of a finite series:

$$\sum_{k=0}^{n} a_k = \sum k = 0^{n-1} a_k + a_n$$

▶ ▶ ▶ **Example 13.7.** Separate off the final term of $\displaystyle\sum_{k=1}^{m} \frac{k}{k+1}$

We do this by only taking the sum to $m - 1$:

$$\sum_{k=1}^{m} \frac{k}{k+1} = \left[\sum_{k=1}^{m-1} \frac{k}{k+1} \right] + \frac{m}{m+1}$$

◀ ◀ ◀

In a **telescoping series**, parts of adjacent terms cancel, so that the total only depends on the first term and the last term.

▶ ▶ ▶ **Example 13.8.** Simplify $\displaystyle\sum_{k=1}^{n} \frac{1}{k(k+1)}$.

Using partial fractions or other algebraic manipulation we can write

$$\frac{1}{k(k+1)} = \frac{1}{k} - \frac{1}{k+1}$$

Hence

$$\sum_{k=1}^{n} \frac{1}{k(k+1)} = \sum_{k=1}^{n} \left(\frac{1}{k} - \frac{1}{k+1} \right)$$

$$= \left[1 - \frac{1}{2}\right] + \left[\frac{1}{2} - \frac{1}{3}\right] + \left[\frac{1}{3} - \frac{1}{4}\right] + \cdots + \left[\frac{1}{n-1} - \frac{1}{n}\right] + \left[\frac{1}{n} - \frac{1}{n+1}\right]$$

$$= 1 - \frac{1}{n+1} = \frac{n}{n+1}$$

We use the upper-case Greek letter Π to denote the product of a sequence, in the same way that we use Σ to denote the sum of a series.

$$\prod_{k=1}^{10} a_k = a_1 a_2 a_3 \cdots a_9 a_{10}$$

▶ ▶ ▶ **Example 13.9.**

$$\prod_{k=3}^{7} \frac{k}{k+3} = \frac{3}{3+3} \cdot \frac{4}{3+4} \cdot \frac{5}{3+5} \cdot \frac{6}{3+6} \cdot \frac{7}{3+7}$$

◀ ◀ ◀

▶ ▶ ▶ **Example 13.10.** $\displaystyle\prod_{k=1}^{n} = 1 \cdot 2 \cdot 3 \cdot 4 \cdots n = n!$ ◀ ◀ ◀

Table 13.1. Useful Properties of Sums and Products

$$\sum_{k=m}^{n} a_k + \sum_{k=m}^{n} b_k = \sum_{k=m}^{n} (a_k + b_k)$$

$$c \sum_{k=m}^{n} a_k = \sum_{k=m}^{n} c a_k$$

$$\left(\prod_{k=m}^{n} a_k\right)\left(\prod_{k=m}^{n} b_k\right) = \prod_{k=m}^{n} (a_k b_k)$$

▶ ▶ ▶ **Example 13.11.** Find the sum of $\displaystyle\sum_{k=3}^{n} \frac{1}{k}$ and $\displaystyle\sum_{k=1}^{n} \frac{1}{k+1}$.

$$\sum_{k=3}^{n} \frac{1}{k} + \sum_{k=1}^{n} \frac{1}{k+1} = \sum_{k=3}^{n} \frac{1}{k} + \frac{1}{1+1} + \frac{1}{2+1} - \sum_{k=3}^{n} \frac{1}{k+1}$$

$$= \sum_{k=3}^{n} \left(\frac{1}{k} + \frac{1}{k+1}\right) + \frac{1}{2} + \frac{1}{3} = \frac{5}{6} + \sum_{k=3}^{n} \frac{2k+1}{k(k+1)}$$

▶ ▶ ▶ **Example 13.12.** Simplify $\prod_{k=1}^{N} 3(k+1)$.

$$\prod_{k=1}^{N} 3(k+1) = 3^N \prod_{k=1}^{N} (k+1)$$
$$= 3^N (2)(3)(4) \cdots (N+1) = 3^N (N+1)!$$

◀ ◀ ◀

One of the most common manipulations that is required when we analyze series is a change of variables. Usually the purpose of a change of variables is to change the start or end index of a sum or product. For example, if we are adding together two nfinite series, and one starts at zero, and the other starts at 1, it is convenient to changes the variable so that they either both start at 0 or both start at 1.

▶ ▶ ▶ **Example 13.13.** Change the variable in the series $\sum_{k=0}^{6} \frac{1}{k+1}$ using the substitution $j = k + 1$.

When $k = 0$, we have $j = 0 + 1 = 1$, the lower index is 1.

When $k = 6$, whe have $j = 6 + 1 = 7$, so the upper index is 7.

Making these substitutions gives

$$\sum_{k=0}^{6} \frac{1}{k+1} = \sum_{j=1}^{7} \frac{1}{j}$$

◀ ◀ ◀

▶ ▶ ▶ **Example 13.14.** Rewrite the sum $\sum_{k=1}^{n+1} \frac{k}{n+k}$ with the variable $j = k - 1$.

When $k = 1$ we have $j = 0$.

When $k = n + 1$ we have $j = n + 1 - 1 = n$.

Making these substitutions gives us

$$\sum_{k=1}^{n+1} \frac{k}{n+k} = \sum_{j=0}^{n} \frac{j+1}{n+j+1} = \sum_{k=0}^{n} \frac{k+1}{n+k+1}$$

◀ ◀ ◀

Geometric and Power Series

A geometric series is any series of the form

$$\sum_{k=0}^{\infty} ar^k = a + ar + ar^2 + ar^3 + ar^4 + \cdots$$

If $|r| > 1$ the terms grow progressively larger and the series diverges. If $|r| < 1$, we can derive a formula for the sum by the following manipulation:

$$S = a + ar + ar^2 + ar^3 + ar^4 + \cdots$$
$$rS = ar + ar^2 + ar^4 + ar^5 + \cdots$$

$$S - rS = a \text{ (subtracting)}$$

Therefore

$$S = \frac{a}{1 - r}$$

▶ ▶ ▶ **Example 13.15.** Find the sum

$$S = 5 - 5/3 + 5/3^2 - 5/3^3 + 5/3^4 + \cdots$$

We have $a = 5$ and $r = -1/3$. Therefore

$$S = \frac{5}{1 - (-1/3)} = \frac{5}{4/3} = \frac{15}{4} = 3.75$$

◀ ◀ ◀

A **power series** is any series of the form

$$f(x) = \sum_{k=0}^{\infty} c_k x^k = c_0 + c_1 x + c_2 x^2 + c_3 x^3 + \cdots$$

where the coefficients $c_0, c_1, \ldots$ are constants. The series is a function of x, which is why we have labeled it as $f(x)$ rather than S. If all the coefficients in a power series are equal to 1 then it becomes

$$f(x) = 1 + x + x^2 + x^3 + \cdots$$

So long as $|x| < 1$, this is a geometric series with $a = 1$ and $r = x$. Finding the sum tells us that

$$\frac{1}{1 - x} = 1 + x + x^2 + x^3 + \cdots$$

Differentiating both sides of the equation gives another series we can sum,

$$\frac{1}{(1-x)^2} = 1 + 2x + 3x^2 + 4x^3 + \cdots$$

Definition 13.3. Generating Function

Let $c_0, c_1, c_2, c_3, \ldots$ be any given sequence. Then any power series of the form

$$\sum_{k=0}^{\infty} c_k^k = c_0 + c_1 x + c_2 x^2 + c_3 x^3 + \cdots$$

is called a **generating function for the sequence** c_k.

▶ ▶ ▶ **Example 13.16.** We have already shown that $1/(1-x)$ is a generating function for $1, 1, 1, 1, \cdots$, and that $1/(1-x)^2$ is a generating function for the sequence $1, 2, 3, 4, \cdots$. ◀ ◀ ◀

If we know a recurrence relation for a sequence sometimes we can use that to help us find a generating function.

▶ ▶ ▶ **Example 13.17.** Find a generating function

$$S = F_0 + F_1 x + F_2 x^2 + F_3 x^3 + F_4 x^4 + \cdots$$

for the Fibonacci sequence.

The trick is to use the recurrence relation $F_n = F_{n-1} + F_{n-2}$, as follows. We subtract xS for the $n-1$ term and $x^2 S$ for the $n-2$ term in the recurrence.

$$S = F_0 + F_1 x + F_2 x^2 + F_3 x^3 + F_4 x^4 + \cdots$$
$$xS = xF_0 + F_1 x^2 + F_2 x^3 + F_3 x^4 + F_4 x^5 + \cdots$$
$$x^2 S = x^2 F_0 + F_1 x^3 + F_2 x^4 + F_3 x^5 + F_4 x^6 + \cdots$$
$$\overline{S - xS - x^2 S = F_0 + (F_1 - F_0)x + (F_2 - F_1 - F_0)x^2 + (F_3 - F_2 - F_1)x^2 +}$$
$$(F_4 - F_3 - F_2)x^3 + \cdots = 1$$

The last step follows because $F_0 = F_1 = 1$ and each subsequent term in parenthesis is of the form $F_n - F_{n-1} - F_{n-2} = 0$ (by the recursion relation that defines the Fibonacci Sequence). Hence the generating function is $1/(1 - x - x^2)$. ◀ ◀ ◀

Representing Sequences in Python

The efficient way to reprsent sequences in Python are with iterators and generators. An iterator is must be defined as a class and must have a __next__ method that tells us how to produce the next element of the sequence. Since coding classes is cumbersome, there is a shorthand version, namely generators. A generator is defined as a function, but instead of a **return** value it has a **yield** value. Consider the Fibonacci sequence defined below in exercise 1. A generator for this can be coded as

```
def fibonacci(N):
    a, b = 0, 1
    while a < N:
        yield a
        a, b = b, a+b
```

For example, to generate and print all the Fibonacci numbers under 100, we would have to first create the generator, and then invoke it:

```
y=fibonacci(100)
for x in y:
    print(x," ",end="")
```

```
0  1  1  2  3  5  8  13  21  34  55  89
```

Once a created instance of a generator has been invoked, it is "used up" in the sense that it cannot be invoked again. A new instance would have to be created.

We could use this technique to create an infinite sequence by setting the upper limit to **float("inf")**. The following creates such an "infinite" sequence, then prints and sums the first 25 members of the sequence:

```
y=fibonacci(float("inf"))
s=0; counter =0
for j in y:
    if counter>=25:
        break
    s+=j
    counter+=1
    print(j," ",end="")
print ()
print (s)
```

```
0   1   1   2   3   5   8   13   21   34   55   89   144   233   377   610
   987   1597   2584   4181   6765   10946   17711   28657   46368
121392
```

Exercises

1. The Fibonacci Sequence is defined by the recurrence $f_0 = 0$, $f_1 = 1$, and $f_n = f_{n-1} + f_{n-2}$ for $n > 1$. Write out the next five members of the Fibonacci Sequence

2. Show that the Fibonacci sequence defined in the previous exercise satisfy $(\varphi^n - (-\varphi)^{-n})/\sqrt{5}$ where $\varphi = (1 + \sqrt{5})/2$.

3. The Catalan number C_n gives the number possible non-intersecting diagonals in a a convex polygon with $2n$ vertices. The formula is

$$C_n = \frac{1}{n+1}\binom{2n}{n} = \frac{(2n)!}{(n+1)!n!}$$

Write out C_1, C_2, C_3, C_4, C_5.

4. Show that the Catalan number C_n satisfies the recurrence relationship

$$(n+1)C_n = (4n-2)C_{n-1}, \ n \geqslant 2,$$

where $C_1=1$.

5. Write a Python generator for the first n Catalan numbers.

14. Cardinality

The concept of **cardinality** is used to measure and compare the **size** of sets. If a set is finite, all we have to do is count the number of elements in the set. If the set contains subsets, we do not count the members of the subsets. We will use the the words size and cardinality interchangeably, and denote the cardinality (or size) of a set S with the absolute value notation $|S|$. We say that sets have the same size if they can be placed in one-one-alignment with one another. Recall from chapter 12 that two sets can be placed in one-to-one alignment if there is a bijection between them.

Definition 14.1. Cardinality

Let S be a finite set that contains n elements. Then we say that the **cardinality** of S is n and we write $|S| = n$. More precisely, $|S| = n$ if and only if there is some bijection $f : S \mapsto \{1, 2, \ldots, n\}$.

Definition 14.2. Same Cardinality (finite sets)

If two sets contain the same number of elements we say that thy have the **same cardinality**. More precisely, let S and T be sets. We say that $|S| = |T|$ if we can find a bijection $f : S \mapsto T$, i.e., S and T can be placed in one-to-one alignment.

▶ ▶ ▶ **Example 14.1.** Let $A = \{1, 7, 9, 4\}$, $B = \{3, 6, \{4, 8, 12\}, 9\}$, and $C = \{A, B\}$.

Then $|A| = 4$, $|B| = 4$, and $|C| = 2$.

To see that $|A| = |B|$. we can define a bijection: $f(1) = 3$; $f(7); = 6$; $f(9) = \{4, 8, 12\}$l $f(4) = 9$. The inverse function if $f^{-1}(3) = 1$; $f^{-1}(6) = 7$; $f^{-1}(\{4, 8, 12\}) = 9$; $f^{-1}(9) = 4$. ◀ ◀ ◀

For infinite sets, we can only define relative cardinality. We use the same definition of same cardinality as before. As we will see, there are many different sizes of infinity. Some infinite sets will turn out to be the same size, while some infinite sets will be infinitely larger than other infinite sets. One of the results of advanced set theory is that infinite sets can be grouped into equivalence classes with increasing cardinality

$$\aleph_0 < \aleph_1 < \aleph_2 < \cdot$$

The integers $\mathbb{Z}$ have cardinality $\aleph_0$, while the real numbers have cardinality $\aleph_1$. The rational numbers have the same cardinality as the integers, somewhat unexpectedly. There are no sets with cardinality between $\aleph_0$ and $\aleph_1$, and it turns out that

$$\aleph_1 = 2^{\aleph_0}$$

The power set of of the integers also has cardinality α_1, but the power set of $\mathbb{R}$ has cardinality

$$\aleph_2 = 2^{\aleph_1} = 2^{2^{\aleph_0}}$$

The increasing sizes of infinity rapidly becomes mind-boggling.

Definition 14.3. Same Cardinality (Infinite Sets)

Let S and T be any two sets. We say that S and T have the same cardinality, and write $|S| = |T|$, if we can find a bijection $f : S \mapsto T$, i.e., S and T can be placed in one-to-one alignment.

An example is given by sets that can be placed in alignment with the positive integers. These sets are called countable or enumerable sets.

Definition 14.4. Enumerable Numbers

Let S be a set. Then if the set can be placed in one-to-one alignment with the positive integers then we say the S is **countable** or **enumerable**, and say that S has cardinality **aleph-null**, which we write as $|S| = \aleph_0$.

One counterintuitive result of this definition is that it is possible to find (many) cases of infinite sets where $Q \subseteq T$ but $|S| = |T|$. All it takes is a bijection.

Theorem 14.1. Cardinality of Positive Integers

The even positive integers are enumerable, i.e., have cardinality $\aleph_0$.

Proof. Let E denote the even positive integers. We need to find a function $f : \mathbb{Z}^+ \mapsto E$ that is (a) 1-1; and (b) onto. Let $f(k) = 2k$.

Proof that f is 1-1.

1. Suppose $p = f(m)$ and $q = f(n)$ for some integers m and n such that $p = q$.
2. By definition of f, $p = 2m$ and $q = 2n$
3. By step 1, $2m = p = q = 2n$.
4. Dividing through by 2, $m = n$. Hence f is 1-1.

Proof that f is onto.

1. Let $p \in E$ be any even number.
2. Since p is even there exists an integer k such that $p = 2k$.
3. By definition of f, we know that $p = f(k)$ for the k found in step 2.
4. Hence for any $p \in E$ there exists $k \in \mathbb{Z}^+$ such that $p = f(k)$. This is the definition of onto.

Since f is both 1-1 and onto, it is a bijection. Thus the positive even numbers and the positive integers have the same cardinality. $\square$

Theorem 14.2. Cardinality of $\mathbb{Z}$

The integers have cardinality $\aleph_0$

The proof of theorem 14.2 is given in exercise 5.

Theorem 14.3. Cardinality of Rational Numbers

The positive rational numbers have cardinality $\aleph_0$.

Figure 14.1.: Arrangement of the positive integers in a grid and assignment of an ordering that places the ordered pairs (i, j) in a one-to-one relationship with $\mathbb{Z}^+$.

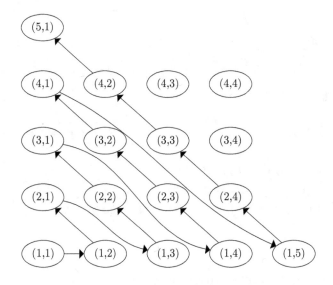

Proof. Arrange the set $\mathbb{Z}^+ \times \mathbb{Z}^+$ on a grid and assign an ordering to the ordered pairs (i, j) as illustrated in figure 14.1. This defines the sequenc

$$a_1 = (1, 1), a_2 = (1, 2), a_3 = (2, 1), a_4 = (1, 3), a_5 = (2, 2), \ldots$$

Next define the sequence b_k by $b_k = a_{k1}/a_{k2}$. The first few elements of the sequence b_k are

$$b_1 = 1$$
$$b_2 = 1/2$$
$$b_3 = 2$$
$$b_4 = 1/3$$
$$b_5 = 2/2 = 1$$
$$b_6 = 3/1 = 3$$
$$b_7 = 1/4$$
$$b_8 = 3/2$$

The function b_k is a bijection.

It is onto because for every positive rational number p/q, there is some ordered pair (p, q) that is defined in a_k, and hence in b_k.

To see that it is 1-1 because let x and y be any two positive rational numbers such that $x = y$. Since x and y are rational numbers there exist integers p, q, r, and s such that $x = p/q$ in reduced form and $y = r/s$ in reduced form. Since $x=y$ then $p/q = r/s$. Since both fractions are in reduced form and they are equal, then $p = r$ and $q = s$. Hence the ordered pairs $(p, q) = (r, s)$ are the same. Therefore both x and y must be matched with the same member of b_k. This shows that b_k is 1-1.

Since b_k is 1-1 and onto, it is a bijection. $\square$

The following theorem is intuitive: we expect that a portion of the whole is smaller than the whole. If we can count something, we should be able to count the size of any portion of if.

Theorem 14.4.

Subsets of countable sets are countable.

Furthermore, if a S is to big to count, we would intuit that anything that includes S as a subset is bigger than S and must also be too big to count.

Theorem 14.5.

Any set with an uncountable subset is uncountable.

Now we need to demonstrate that the real numbers form a bigger set than the integers.

Theorem 14.6. Uncountability of Reals

The real numbers are not countable.

Proof. Proof by contradiction. Suppose that the real numbers between 0 and 1 are countable. Then we can enumerate them as decimals. Let x_{jn} be the nth decimal digit of the jth real number. The enumeration can be written something like this.

$$x_1 = 0.x_{11}x_{12}x_{13} \cdots x_{1n} \cdots$$
$$x_2 = 0.x_{21}x_{22}x_{23} \cdots x_{2n} \cdots$$
$$x_3 = 0.x_{31}x_{32}x_{33} \cdots x_{3n} \cdots$$
$$\vdots$$

Now define the sequence of digits y_n as follows:

$$y_k = \begin{cases} 1, & \text{if } x_{kk} = 0 \\ 0, & \text{if } x_{kk} \neq 0 \end{cases}$$

Here x_{kk} is the kth digit of the kth real number. These digits are found by proceeding down the diagonal of the enumeration. This definition ensures that $y_k \neq x_{kk}$. Let

$$y = 0.y_1y_2y_3 \cdots y_n \cdots$$

The number y has been constructed so that y is not equal to any number in the enumeration:

$$y_1 \neq x_{11} \Rightarrow y \neq x_1$$
$$y_2 \neq x_{22} \Rightarrow y \neq x_2$$
$$y_3 \neq x_{33} \Rightarrow y \neq x_3$$
$$\vdots$$
$$y_n \neq x_{nn} \Rightarrow y \neq x_n$$
$$\vdots$$

Thus we have constructed a real number in the interval from 0 to 1 that is not in the enumeration. This contradicts the assumption that we can enumerate the list all possible real real numbers in the interval from 0 to 1. Hence the interval [0,1] is uncountable.

The interval from 0 to 1 is a subset of $\mathbb{R}$. By theorem 14.5, the real numbers are uncountable. $\square$

Exercises

1. Prove that cardinality is reflexive, i.e., show that a set has the same cardinality as itself.

2. Prove that cardinality is transitive, i.e., show that if $|A| = |B|$ and $|B| = |C|$ then $|A| = |C|$.

3. Prove that the positive odd integers are countable.

4. Prove that set of all even integers is countable.

5. Prove that the integers have the same cardinality as the positive integers (theorem 14.2). Hint: Let $f : \mathbb{Z}^+ \mapsto \mathbb{Z}$, where $f(k) = k/2$ if k is even, and $f(k) = (1 - k)/2$ if k is odd.

6. Prove theorem 14.5. Hint: consider the contrapositive of theorem 14.4.

15. Counting

We frequently want to enumerate (write out) a sequence or list of integers from m to n, where $m \leqslant n$. In Python we do this with the **range** function

```
list(range(m,n+1))
```

In Python 3 we must cast the **range** as a **list** if we actually want to print it out, because Python 3 does not actually evaluate the values of a **range** object until they are actually needed. This saves space for very large **range**'s that may not be used.

```
print(prange(5,11))
```

```
range(5,11)
```

```
print(list(range(5,11))
```

```
[5, 6, 7, 8, 9, 10]
```

```
for j in range(5,11):
    print("{:3d}".format(j),end="")
```

```
  5   6   7   8   9  10
```

We can formally define a range as a sequence consisting of the integers between two integers m and n. The length of this sequence is $n - m + 1$.

Theorem 15.1.

Let $m, n \in \mathbb{Z}$ where $m \leqslant n$ and define the **range** set $R(m, n)$ by

$$R(m, n) = \{m, m + 1, m + 2, \ldots, n\}$$

Then

$$|R(m, n)| = n - m + 1$$

Proof. Prove by induction on n.

Basis Step. If $n = m$ then $R(m, n) = \{m\}$, which contains precisely one element. since $n - m + 1 = 1$, the theorem holds for $n = m$.

Inductive Hypothesis. Let $n = k \geqslant m$ and assume that

$$|R(m, k)| = k - m + 1$$

We need to show that

$$|R(m, k + 1)| = k + 1 - m + 1 = k - m + 2$$

Inductive Proof. The range set $R(m, k + 1)$ is

$$\begin{aligned}
R(m, k + 1) &= \{m, m + 1, \ldots, k - 1, k, k + 1\} \\
&= \{m, m + 1, \ldots, k - 1, k\} \cup \{k + 1\} \\
&= R(m, k) \cup \{k + 1\}
\end{aligned}$$

By the inductive hypothesis, the first set has $k - m + 1$ elements in it. The second set has precisely one element in it.

Since $k + 1 \notin R(m, k)$ we must add precisely one element to $R(m, k)$ to produce $R(m, k + 1)$. Hence

$$|R(m, k + 1)| = |R(m, k)| + 1 = (k - m + 1) + 1 = k - m + 2$$

as required. $\square$

▶▶▶ **Example 15.1.** The number of elements in an array $A[5], A[6], \ldots,$ $A[23]$ is 23-5+1 = 17. ◀ ◀ ◀

Possibility Trees

It is sometimes useful to describe possibilities by a tree. An example is given by a tournament such as the world series, where one two teams play additional games until one team has won four games. An example is given in figure 15.1 where two competitors must win two rounds to win the tour-

---

nament. We can visualize the possible ways that each competitor can win by looking at the pathways to each winner; we can count the ways that each competitor can win by counting the leafs that contain the winner's name. In figure 15.1, there are six leaf nodes. Venus can win if the sequence of winners is Venus/Venus, Venus/Serena/Venus, or Serena/Venus/Venus. Serena wins if the sequence Serena/Serena, Venus/Serena/Serena, or Serena/Venus/Serena.

Figure 15.1.: The winners in a best-of-three coding playoff between the two finalists are shown in successive levels of a possibility tree. The name of the winner at each round is given in the box. Once a particular candidate has won two rounds, she has won the tournament and the tree needs to descend no further. Tournament winners are indicated by a (W).

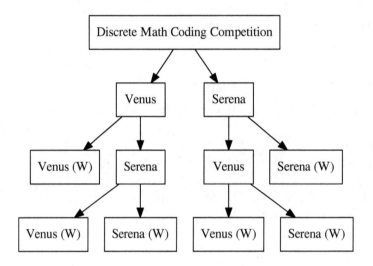

A decision tree can also be used to show the different ways objects can be combined. Suppose Joe hates it when his socks and his shirt are the same color. Joe has three colors of socks (white, red, and blue) and four colors of shirts (black, white, green, and pink). Figure 15.2 illustrates Joe's decision tree for getting dressed. The total number of shirt/socks combinations is found by counting the leaves. There are 12 leaves in this example. The wardrobe combinations are found by tracing the path from the start node to the leaf. If Joe wants to ensure that socks and his shirt are different colors, he needs to avoid the white socks / white shirt path. Since there are 12 leaves total that means he has a chance of 11/12 or about a 91.6% chance of picking socks and shirt that are not the same color if he chooses them randomly (assuming his shirts and socks are uniformly distributed).

Figure 15.2.: A decision tree (the root in the center) showing the number of ways Joe can select his shirt and his socks in the morning.

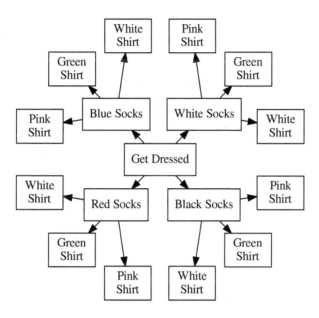

We observe that in Joe's closet, with 4 colors of socks and 3 colors of shirt, there were $3 \times 4 = 12$ wardrobe combinations. This multiplication rule can be extended to as many different steps are required to complete the entire process: to get the total number of possibilities, multiply the total number of cases at each step.

Theorem 15.2. Multiplication Rule

If some process consists of n steps such that
  1. The first step can be performed in k_1 ways;
  2. The second step can be performed in k_2 ways;
  3. The third step can be performed in k_3 ways;
   $\vdots$
  n. The nth step can be performed in k_n ways;
and the number of ways each step can be performed does not depend on any of the other steps, then the entire operation can be performed in $k_1 k_2 \cdots k_n$ steps.

▶ ▶ ▶ **Example 15.2.** Suppose you run a company that builds laptop computers. You give the customer the following choices:

1. Choice of four different CPU's (i3/i5/i7/i7(turbo));
2. Choice of six different operating systems (Windows Home, Premium, Ultimate, Ubuntu Linux, Fedora Linux, Linux Mint);
3. Choice of five different Memory sizes (4/8/12/16/32 GB);
4. Choice of six storage options (250/500 GB or 250/500/1TB/2TB SSD);
5. Choice of two different screen sizes (13 inch, 15 inch);
6. Choice of three different screen types (Normal/Glossy/Touch Screen);
7. Choice of three different case colors (Black/Silver/Gold);
8. Choice of two different video cards (Normal/Turbo);
9. Choice of two different wireless cards (2.6/5 GHZ);
10. Choice of internal optical (DVD/BluRay) or extra HD (5 options);
11. Choice of battery (4/12 hour charge)
12. Choice of basic warranty (1/2/3 year) or basic plus damage protection (1/2/3 year)

How many different configurations does the company sell?

None of the options in any step depends on what we have chosen in any of the other steps. Therefore when using the multiplication rule, we are allowed to multiply the number of choices allowed in each step to determine the total:

$$n = 4 \times 6 \times 5 \times 6 \times 2 \times 3 \times 3 \times 2 \times 2 \times 7 \times 2 \times 6 = 4,354,560$$

◀ ◀ ◀

▶ ▶ ▶ **Example 15.3.** What does the following block of code do?

```
for i in range(1,4):
    for j in range(5,10):
        for k in range(15,35):
            print("Hello World!",end="")
```

The first loop performs $4 - 1 + 1 = 4$ iterations.

The j loop performs $10 - 5 + 1 = 6$ iterations.

The k loop performs $35 - 15 + 1 = 21$ iterations.

The code block will print "Hello World!" $4 \times 6 \times 21 = 504$ times. ◀ ◀ ◀

The multiplication rule must be applied with care, however. If choices are conditional upon one another then the calculation will depend on the order in which the choices are made.

▶ ▶ ▶ **Example 15.4.** Suppose a group of four individuals, Andrea (A), Becky (B), Cody (C) and Damien (D), go out to dinner together to celebrate Andrea's 20th birthday. Becky is 21, Cody is 21 and Damien is 22. They need to make their meal selections. To get a special birthday discount at the restaurant there are some restrictions:

1. One person must buy a steak, seafood, and beer combo. Since this meal includes a beer it must go to someone over 21, i.e., either Becky, Cody or Damien.
2. One person must buy a steak combo, but Andrea and Becky don't like steak, so this must be either Cody or Damien.
3. One person must buy a seafood combo.
4. Everyone else eats at the buffet bar.

How many ways can we choose the different meal orders?

If we choose who orders the steak combo first, then we choose who orders the steak and seafood combo, then finally we choose who orders the seafood combo, the multiplication rule gives us the following answer:

$$N = (\text{steak}) \times (\text{steak \& seafood}) \times (\text{seafood})$$
$$= (2 \ (\text{C or D})) \times (2 \ (\text{Any except A and not already ordered}))$$
$$\times (2 \ (\text{whoever is left})) = 8$$

The decision tree for this ordering is shown in figure 15.3; the tree is completely balanced and there are eight leaves. If instead we first choose who orders the steak and seafood combo, then we choose who orders the seafood combo, then choose who orders the steak combo last, we get this answer:

$$N = (3 \ (\text{any except A}) \ ) \times (3 \ (\text{Any except whoever ordered S \& S}))$$
$$\times (2 \ (\text{either C or D})) = 18$$

The problem is that our choices are not balanced. For example, in the third factor, one of C or D might have ordered Steak & Seafood, and one of them might have ordered Seafood. so we should not always count 2 there. We can see from the decision tree (figure 15.4) that two pathways lead to dead ends and the tree is not perfectly balanced.   ◀ ◀ ◀

Counting Sets

If a set can be decomposed into non-overlapping (non-intersecting) subsets, then the size of the original set is equal to the sum of the sizes of subsets.

Figure 15.3.: Decision tree for the first ordering of choices in example 4.

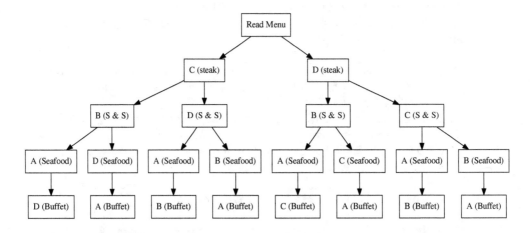

Figure 15.4.: Decision tree for the second ordering of choices in example 4.

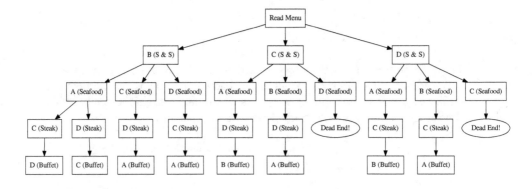

Theorem 15.3. Addition Rule

Let A be any finite set such that $A = \bigcup_{i=1}^{n} A_i$, where the A_i are disjoint, i.e., $A_i \cap A_j = \emptyset$ for $i \neq j$. Then

$$|A| = \sum_{i=1}^{n} |A_i|$$

▶ ▶ ▶ **Example 15.5.** Find the number of passwords that can be composed of 6, 7 or 8 characters A-Z,a-z,0-9 and the special character #, ^,?, and $.

There are $2 \times 26 + 10 + 4 = 66$ different characters.

$$|\{\text{passwords})\}| = |\{\text{6-character-passwords}\}| + |\{\text{6-character-passwords}\}| +$$
$$|\{\text{8-character-passwords}\}|$$
$$= 66^6 + 66^7 + 66^8 \approx 3.66578 \times 10^{14} \quad \square$$

◀ ◀ ◀

▶ ▶ ▶ **Example 15.6.** How many integers between 0 and 999 are divisible by 5?

A number is divisible by 5 if it ends in zero or if it ends in 5. If X is any digit 0 to 9, inclusive, a three digit number (possibly with leading zeros) can be written as XXX. Define

$$A_0 = \{\text{3 digit numbers of the form } XX0\}$$
$$A_5 = \{\text{3 digit numbers of the form } XX5\}$$

We are interested in finding $|A_0 \cup A_5|$. We can use the addition rule since $A_0 \cap A_5 = \varnothing$. In each set, there are ten different ways we can fill out the X's. Thus

$$|A_0| = 10 \times 10 = 100$$
$$|A_5| = 10 \times 10 = 100$$
$$|A_0 \cup A_5| = |A_0| + |A_5| = 100 + 100 = 200$$

There are 200 numbers between 0 and 999 that are divisible by 5. ◀ ◀ ◀

The formula for the size of a set different is intuitive. If you remove a subset from a larger set, the size of the larger set is reduced by the number of items in the smaller set.

Theorem 15.4. Difference Rule

Let A be any finite and let $B \subseteq A$. Then

$$|A - B| = |A| - |B|$$

▶ ▶ ▶ **Example 15.7.** How many 4-number PIN'S (Personal Information Numbers) have repeated characters?

Let

$$A = \text{Set of 4 number PINS with repeated characters allowed}$$

B = Set of 4 number PINS without any repeated characters

C = Set of 4 number PINS with repeated characters = $A - B$

Then by the multiplication rule,

$$|A| = 10^4 = 10,000$$
$$|B| =_{10} P_4 = \frac{10!}{(10-4)!} = 10 \cdot 9 \cdot 8 \cdot 7 = 5040$$
$$|C| = |A| - |B| = 10,000 - 5040 = 4960$$

◀ ◀ ◀

Theorem 15.5. Inclusion/Exclusion Rule

Let A and B be any finite sets. Then

$$|A \cup B| = |A| + |B| - |A \cap B|$$

If C is also a finite set, then

$$|A \cup B \cup C| = |A| + |B| + |C| - |A \cap B| - |A \cap C| - |B \cap C| + |A \cap B \cap C|$$

▶ ▶ ▶ **Example 15.8.** How many integers $1 \leqslant x \leqslant 1000$ are multiples of either 3 or 5?

Let A and B be the sets of all multiples of 3 and 5, respectively. Then by the inclusion/exclusion rule,

$$|A \cup B| = |A| + |B| - |A \cap B|$$

But

$$|A| = |\{3, 6, 9, \ldots, 999\}| = 333$$
$$|B| = |\{5, 10, 15, \ldots, 1000\}| = 200$$
$$|A \cap B| = |\{15, 30, 45, \ldots, 990 = 66 \cdot 15\}| = 66$$

Hence $|A \cup B| = 333 + 200 - 66 = 467$.

Permutations

Sometimes we are not just interested in the elements of a set. We are also interested in using the elements in a specific order. For example, in a

---

kindergarten class of 12 students, how many different ways can the students line up? At a table of five people in a restaurant, in how many different orders can a server take the diners' orders? If we need to go shopping at 3 different stores on the way home from work, in how many different ways can we order our choice of stops? The answers to of these questions is the number of permutations of a sets of 12, 5, and 3 items, respectively.

Definition 15.1. Permutation

A **permutation** of a set is a specific ordering of the elements in the set.

▶ ▶ ▶ **Example 15.9.** The possible permutations of the set $\{a, b, c\}$ are:
$$abc, acb, bac, bca, cab, cba$$

◀ ◀ ◀

Suppose a set has n distinct items in it. We want to calculate the number of ways we can permute (rearrange) those n items. We obtain this number P_n using the multiplication rule.

- There are n ways to select the first item.
- Once the first item has been removed, there are $n - 1$ ways to pick the second item.
- Once the first two items have been removed, there are $n - 2$ ways to pick the third item.
- Repeat this process and keep choosing new items until no items are left. Each time we select an an item, there is one fewer items left to select from for the next choice.
- Applying the multiplication item,

$$P_n = n(n - 1)(n - 2)(n - 3) \cdots 3 \cdot 2 \cdot 1 = n!$$

Theorem 15.6. Permutations of a Set

The number of permutations of a set with n distinct elements is $n!$

Sometimes we don't want to pick the entire set. We might want to pick some smaller subset. For example, in a kindergarten class of 12 students,

---

how may ways can we pick out 5 students and line them up in order. This is called an r-permutation. We denote it by $_nP_r$, the number of permutations of n things taken r at a time.

Definition 15.2. r-permutation

An **r-permutation** of a set with n elements is an ordered selection of r elements from the set of n elements. The total number of permutations of length r from a set of length n is denoted by $_nP_r$.

To determine the number of r-permutations a set of n distinct items, we apply the same process we did to calculate the total number of permutations of a set of n items. However, instead of counting down until there are no items left, we stop when we have selected our r^{th} item.

- There are n ways to select the first item.
- Once the first item has been removed, there are $n-1$ ways to pick the second item.
- Once the first two items have been removed, there are $n-2$ ways to pick the third item.
- Repeat this process and keep choosing new items until r items have been selected. Each time we select an an item, there is one fewer items left to select from for the next choice.
- Applying the multiplication item,

$$P_n = n(n-1)(n-2)(n-3)\cdots(n-r+1) = \frac{n!}{(n-r)!}$$

Theorem 15.7. Number of r-permutations of a set

$$_nP_r = \frac{n!}{(n-r)!}$$

▶▶▶ **Example 15.10.** Prove that for all integers $n \geqslant 2$, $_nP_2 + _nP_1 = n^2$.

Proof. Let $n \geqslant 2$ be an integer. Then

$$_nP_2 + _n P_1 = \frac{n!}{(n-2)!} + \frac{n!}{(n-1)!}$$

$$= n(n-1) + n$$
$$= n^2 - n + n = n^2$$

□

◀ ◀ ◀

We can list out all the r-permutations of a set in Python with **itertools.permutations**.

```
import itertools
c=itertools.permutations(range(5),2)
print(list(c))
```

```
[(0, 1), (0, 2), (0, 3), (0, 4), (1, 0), (1, 2), (1, 3),
(1, 4), (2, 0), (2, 1), (2, 3), (2, 4), (3, 0), (3, 1),
(3, 2), (3, 4), (4, 0), (4, 1), (4, 2), (4, 3)]
```

While it is possible to calculate $_nP_r$ either by listing all the permutations of sets of integers and counting them, or by evaluating the formula using **math.factorial**, we can also determine the value of $_nC_r$ without actually evaluating all the permutations if we use **scipy.special.perm**, which returns $_nC_r$ as a floating point number. This has the advantage of avoiding both the generation of large lists and the division of large factorials.

```
from scipy.special import comb
print(comb(10,5))
```

```
252.0
```

Combinations

Sometimes we are only interested in the different ways we can form a subset, such as how many different ways we can form a basketball team of size 5 from a kindergarten class of size 12. The order in which we choose people doesn't matter: team [Tom, Becky, Andy, Jessica, Bob] is the same as team [Becky, Andy, Bob, Jessica, Tom]. Thus this is not a permutation, because the order in which we have written the names is different. The **combination** of names, however, is the same.

Theorem 15.8. Combinations

Let $n \geqslant r$ be non-negative integers. The number of subsets of size r from a set of size n elements is called the **number of combinations of n items chosen r at a time**. It is denoted by $_nC_r$ or $\binom{n}{r}$, which are read as "n choose r," and is given by the formula

$$_nC_r = \binom{n}{r} = \frac{n!}{(n-r)!r!} = \frac{_nP_r}{r!}$$

▶ ▶ ▶ **Example 15.11.** How may ways can you choose a team of 5 players from a group of 12 people?

$$\binom{12}{5} = \frac{12!}{5!7!} = \frac{12 \cdot 11 \cdot \cancel{10} \cdot 9 \cdot 8 \cdot \cancel{7!}}{\cancel{5} \cdot 4 \cdot 3 \cdot \cancel{2} \cdot 1 \cdot \cancel{7!}} = \frac{\cancel{12} \cdot 11 \cdot 9 \cdot 8}{\cancel{12}} = 792$$

◀ ◀ ◀

▶ ▶ ▶ **Example 15.12.** Suppose that in example 11 that there are two people (A and B) who insist on either both being on the team or both being off the team. How many ways can we choose the team now?

If both A and B are on the team, then the team is ABXXX. There are three slots to fill. Hence we only have to choose combinations of size 3 from the remaining 10 people. In this case we have

$$|\text{teams with A and B}| = \binom{10}{3} = \frac{10!}{3!7!} = \frac{10 \cdot 9 \cdot 8}{6} = 120$$

If neither A nor B are on the team, then we must choose 5 people from the

---

remaining 10, so

$$|\text{teams without A or B}| = \binom{10}{5} = \frac{10!}{5!5!}$$

$$= \frac{\cancel{10} \cdot 9 \cdot 8 \cdot 7 \cdot 6 \cdot \cancel{5!}}{\cancel{5} \cdot 4 \cdot 3 \cdot \cancel{2} \cdot \cancel{5!}} = \frac{3024}{12} = 252$$

Therefore the answer is $120 + 252 = 372$. ◀ ◀ ◀

▶ ▶ ▶ **Example 15.13.** Repeat example 11, but this time suppose that A and B refuse to work together.

Let T_A be the collection of teams that have A but not B; T_B be the collection of teams that have B but not A; and let T_C be the collection of teams that have neither A nor B. These three sets are mutually exclusive, so we can use the addition rule. Since we found $|T_C| = 252$ in example 12. the answer is

$$N = |T_A| + |T_B| + |T_C| = \binom{10}{4} + \binom{10}{4} + 252$$

$$= 210 + 210 + 252 = 672$$

◀ ◀ ◀

▶ ▶ ▶ **Example 15.14.** Repeat example 13 using the difference rule.

Let S_{all} be the collection of all possible teams; S_{AB} the collection of all teams with both A and B on them; and let S_{neither} be the collection of all teams with neither A nor B. Then

$$S_{\text{neither}} = S_{\text{all}} - S_{\text{AB}}$$

Therefore by the set difference rule,

$$|S_{\text{neither}}| = |S_{\text{all}}| - |S_{\text{AB}}| = \binom{12}{5} - \binom{10}{3} = 792 - 120 = 672$$

◀ ◀ ◀

▶ ▶ ▶ **Example 15.15.** Find the number of distinguishable permutations of the letters in the word SYLLABUS.

The word has 8 letters, but not all 8! permutations are distinguishable, because there are two S's and two L's, and if you interchange the L's or interchange the S's, you can't tell the permutations apart.

Starting with an 8-character field, there are $\binom{8}{2} = \frac{8!}{6!2!} = 28$ possible locations for for each of the $L's$.

In the remaining 6-characters, there are $\binom{6}{2} = \frac{6!}{4!2!} = 15$ possible locations for each of the $S's$.

There are 4!=24 possible permutations of the remaining letters Y,A,B,U.

Hence $N = 28 \times 15 \times 24 = 10,080$ possible permutations. ◀ ◀ ◀

Theorem 15.9. Distinguishable Permutations

Suppose that n items are partitioned into
n_1 indistinguishable items of type 1
n_2 indistinguishable items of type 2
...
n_k indistinguishable items of type k
Such that $n_1 + n_2 + \cdots + n_k = n$, then the number of distinct permutations is

$$\binom{n}{n_1} \times \binom{n-n_1}{n_1} \times \binom{n-n_1-n_2}{n_3} \times \cdots \times \binom{n-n_1-n_2-\cdots-n_{k-1}}{n_k}$$

$$= \frac{n!}{n_1! n_2! n_3! \cdots n_k!}$$

▶ ▶ ▶ **Example 15.16.** In example 15, we have $n = 8$, $n_1 = n_2 = 2$ and $n_3 = n_4 = n_5 = n_6 = 1$, so that the total number of permutations is

$$\frac{8!}{2!2!1!1!1!1!} = \frac{8!}{4} = \frac{40,320}{4} = 10,080$$

◀ ◀ ◀

Theorem 15.10. Multisets

The number of ways that r items can be chosen from n categories is

$$\binom{r+n-1}{r}$$

when repetition is allowed.

▶ ▶ ▶ **Example 15.17.** How many different subsets of length 3 can be found in the list [1,2,3,4]?

According to theorem 15.10, the number of subsets is

$$\binom{4+3-1}{3} = \binom{6}{3} == \frac{6!}{3!3!} = \frac{\cancel{6} \cdot 5 \cdot 4 \cdot \cancel{3!}}{\cancel{3!} \cdot \cancel{3!}} = 20$$

Ch. 15. Counting

To verify that this is correct, we can easily list all the possibilities:

$$
\begin{array}{cccc}
111 & 112 & 113 & 114 \\
122 & 123 & 124 & 133 \\
134 & 144 & 222 & 223 \\
224 & 233 & 234 & 244 \\
333 & 334 & 344 & 444
\end{array}
$$

Note that indistinguishable combinations like 113 and 131 are only counted once. ◀ ◀ ◀

Table 15.1. Permutations and Combinations

$$
{}_nP_r = \frac{n!}{(n-r)!}
$$

$$
\binom{n}{n} = 1
$$

$$
\binom{n}{n-1} = n
$$

$$
\binom{n}{n-2} = \frac{n(n-1)}{2}
$$

$$
{}_nC_r = \binom{n}{r} = \binom{n}{n-r}
$$

$$
\binom{n+1}{r} = \binom{n}{r-1} + \binom{n}{r} \quad \text{(Pascal's Formula)}
$$

$$
\sum_{k=0}^{n} \binom{n}{k} a^{n-k} b^k = (a+b)^n \quad \text{(Binomial Theorem)}
$$

In Python we can count the number of combinations ${}_nC_k = \binom{n}{k}$ using **scipy.special.comb**. However, **scipy** returns the the answer as a floating point value and not an integer:

```
import scipy
print(scipy.special.comb(10,5))
```

252.0

You can list out all the possible combinations with **itertools.combinations**.

```
c=list(itertools.combinations(range(10),5))
print(c)
```

```
[(0, 1, 2, 3, 4), (0, 1, 2, 3, 5), (0, 1, 2, 3, 6),
(0, 1, 2, 3, 7), (0, 1, 2, 3, 8), (0, 1, 2, 3, 9),
(0, 1, 2, 4, 5), (0, 1, 2, 4, 6), (0, 1, 2, 4, 7),
.. <output omitted> .. (5, 6, 7, 8, 9)]
```

You can also find the value of $_nC_r$ by calculating the length of the list:

```
c=list(itertools.combinations(range(10),5))
n=len(c)
print(n)
```

252

It also works on strings,

```
list(itertools.combinations("ABCD",2))
```

```
[('A', 'B'), ('A', 'C'), ('A', 'D'), ('B', 'C'), ('B', 'D'),
('C', 'D')]
```

To turn the tuples into lists, we can map a concatenation function through the iterable.

```
list(map(lambda x:x[0]+x[1],
    itertools.combinations("ABCD",2)))
```

```
['AB', 'AC', 'AD', 'BC', 'BD', 'CD']
```

Exercises

1. Build a tree showing the number of ways it is possible to pick a 4-character password out of upper case letters A-Z and the numbers 0-9.

2. You have 12 shirts, 4 pairs of slacks, 14 pairs of socks, and 4 pairs of shoes. How many outfits can you put together?

3. How may different ways can you pick a committee of 4 people from a group of ten?

4. A teacher makes her students stand in line for a field trip. If there are 17 students in the class, how many different ways can the line be arranged?

5. Suppose a kindergarten class of 20 is grouped into five study groups of 4. How many different ways can the groups be selected?

6. There are five classrooms and four classes being offered at the same time. How many different ways can the classes be placed in the different classrooms?

7. Write a decision tree for the baseball world series, where a team must win 4 games to win the series.

8. Use Python to find all combinations of letters of length 4 that are taken from the string "SYLLABUS" and which do not have any characters duplicated.

9. How many bijective mappings are them between two finite sets, where each set contains 5 elements?

10. How many onto mappings $f : A \mapsto B$, where $|A| = 5$ and $|B| = 4$, are possible?

11. How many edges does a complete graph with n vertices have? (See chapter 19.)

12. What is the maximum number of edges in a bipartite graph if there are m and n vertices, respectively, in each of the two halves of the graph? (See chapter 19 for a definition of a bipartite graph.)

16 . Recurrence Relations

In a **recurrence relation**, a function over the integers a_n is defined in terms of earlier values of the argument. A well known recurrence is given by the *Fibonacci Sequence*:

$$a_0 = 1$$
$$a_1 = 1$$
$$a_n = a_{n-1} + a_{n-2} \qquad \text{for } n = 2, 3, \dots$$

This leads to the sequence $\{1, 1, 2, 3, 5, 8, 11, \dots\}$. Recurrence relations are often used to describe mathematical functions, such as the factorial function:

$$a_0 = 1$$
$$a_n = n a_{n-1} \qquad \text{for } n = 1, 2, \dots$$

Recurrences are mathematical descriptions of recursive functions. Any recursive program can be implemented iteratively, although the implementation is sometimes less elegant (although sometimes it is much simpler). Similarly, recursion relations can usually be solved to give explicit formulas for a_n that do not depend on earlier values of a_n. For example, the solution of the factorial sequence is $a_n = n! = 1 \cdot 2 \cdot 3 \cdots n$.

An application of recurrences is given the *Towers of Hanoi* game. In this game, there are three pegs, with a collection n of differently sized disks on the pegs. Initially, the disks are arranged from largest (on the bottom) to smallest (on the top) on peg 1, while pegs 2 and 3 are empty. The goal is to move the n disks to another peg subject to the following rules:

1. We are allowed to move one disk at a time.
2. We cannot put a disk on top of a smaller disk.

We can use recurrences to describe the process of solving the game.

▶ ▶ ▶ **Example 16.1.** Find a recurrence relation for T_n, the minimum number of moves required to move a stack from one peg to another in the Towers of Hanoi game.

The simplest cases are $T_0 = 0$, $T_1 = 1$, $T_2 = 3$ (exercise 2).

Here is a general solution. Label the pegs A, B, C, and suppose all the disks are on peg A initially.

1. Transfer $n - 1$ disks to an empty peg B (T_{n-1} moves).
2. Transfer n^{th} disk to empty peg C (one move)
3. Transfer all the disks from peg B to peg C (another T_{n-1} moves)

The total number of moves is thus $T_n = 2T_{n-1} + 1$. ◀ ◀ ◀

▶ ▶ ▶   **Example 16.2.**   Find a pattern in the sequence in values for the Towers of Hanoi game, and use it predict a solution. Then prove that the solution is correct.

The first few iterations for T_n give $T_0 = 0$, $T_1 = 1$, $T_2 = 3$, $T_3 = 7$, $T_4 = 15$, $T_5 = 31$, $T_6 = 63$, etc. The pattern *appears to be* $T_n = 2^n - 1$.

Proof. Proof is by induction.

Basis: For $n = 1$, $2^1 - 1 = 2 - 1 = 1 = T_1$, as required.

Inductive Hypothesis: Suppose that $T_n = 2^n - 1$.

We need to show that the formula works for $n+1$, i.e., $T_{n+1} = 2^{n+1} - 1$. From the recurrence relation,

$$
\begin{aligned}
T_{n+1} &= 2T_n + 1 \\
&= 2(2^n - 1) + 1 \qquad \text{by the inductive hypothesis} \\
&= 2^{n+1} - 2 + 1 \\
&= 2^{n+1} - 1
\end{aligned}
$$

as required.   □

Sometimes we can track the pattern of the sequence and use this pattern to postulate an explicit solution to the recurrence, as illustrated for the Towers of Hanoi in example 2. Although we obtained the correct solution in the first part of example 2, there is no guarantee that we have found the correct pattern, even if it looks good for a large number of manually tested examples. We must allways verify it by proof, as we did in the second part of example 2 because the pattern can be misleading.

Most of the time the pattern is not so obvious, and we need to resort to other methods to solve the recurrence. If the recurrence is linear, we can solve the recurrence exactly by finding its **characteristic equation**.

Definition 16.1. Homogeneous Linear Recurrence Relation

A **homogeneous linear recurrence** has the form

$$a_n + c_{n-1}a_{n-1} + c_{n-2}a_{n-2} + \cdots + c_{n-k}a_{n-k} = 0$$

where $c_k \neq 0$, for some $k > 0$. Here k is called the **degree** of the recurrence.

The **characteristic equation** of the recurrence is the polynomial

$$x^n + c_{n-1}x^{n-2} + c_{n-2}x^{n-2} + \cdots + c_{n-k} = 0$$

The solution of a homogeneous linear recurrence is determined by the roots of its characteristic equation. We illustrate this for a **second degree recurrence**, which in its most general form can be written as by(in

$$a_n + ba_{n-1} + ca_{n-2} = 0$$

where b and c are real numbers. (It is possible to define recurrences involving complex numbers but that is beyond our scope.) The corresponding characteristic equation is

$$x^2 + bx + c = 0$$

The roots are
$$x = \frac{-b \pm \sqrt{b^2 - 4c}}{2}$$

There may either be a pair of distinct, real roots (if $b^2 > 4c$); or a a pair of repeated roots (if $b^2 = 4c$); or a complex conjugate pair (if $b^2 < 4c$).

If the roots $x_1 \neq x_2$ are distinct and real, any expression of the form $a_n = x_i^n, i = 1, 2$ is a solution of the recursion. Furthermore, for *any* constants C_1 and C_2, a general solution of the second order equation is

$$a_n = C_1 x_1^n + C_2 x_2^n$$

▶ ▶ ▶ **Example 16.3.** Solve

$$a_0 = 1$$

$$a_1 = 2$$
$$a_n - 5a_{n-1} + 6a_{n-2} = 0$$

We can solve this using the method of characteristic equations. The characteristic equation is

$$0 = x^2 - 5x + 6 = (x-3)(x-2)$$

There are two distinct roots, $x = 3$ and $x = 2$, so the general solution is

$$a_n = C_1 3^n + C_2 2^n$$

We can determine values for C_1 and C_2 by substituting the given $a_0 = 1$ and $a_1 = 2$:

$$1 = a_0 = C_1 + C_2$$
$$2 = a_1 = 3C_1 + 2C_2$$

If we multiply the first equation by 2 and subtract it from the second equation we get

$$0 = C_1$$

Back substitution into either equation gives $C_2 = 1$. Hence the solution to the recurrence is

$$a_n = 2^n$$

If $b^2 = 4c$, then there is only root to the characteristic equation, $x = -b/2$. In this case both $a_n = x^n$ and $a_n = nx^n$ are solutions to the recurrence, and a general solution is

$$a_n = C_1 x^n + C_2 n x^n$$

▶ ▶ ▶ **Example 16.4.** Solve

$$a_0 = 1$$
$$a_1 = 1$$
$$a_n - 6a_{n-1} + 9a_{n-2} = 0$$

The characteristic equation is

$$0 = x^2 - 6x + 9 = (x-3)^2$$

This is a perfect square, with a repeated root of $x = 3$. Thus both 3^n and $n3^n$ are solutions. A general solutions is

$$a_n = C_1 3^n + C_2 n 3^n$$

Using the given values of $a_0 = 1$ and $a_1 = 1$ gives two equations in two unknowns.

$$1 = a_0 = C_1$$
$$1 = a_1 = 3C_1 + 3C_2 = 3 + 3C_2 \Rightarrow C_2 = -2/3$$

and therefore $a_n = 3^n\left[1 - \dfrac{2n}{3}\right]$ is the solution. ◄ ◄ ◄

▶ ▶ ▶ **Example 16.5.**   Verify that $a_n = 3^n\left[1 - \dfrac{2n}{3}\right]$ is a solution of the recurrence in example 4 by direct substitution.

For $n = 0$, the formula gives $a_0 = 3^0\left[1 - \dfrac{2\cdot 0}{3}\right] = 1$ as required.

For $n = 1$, the formula gives $a_1 = 3^1\left[1 - \dfrac{2\cdot 1}{3}\right] = 3\cdot\dfrac{1}{3} = 1$ as required.

For $n \geqslant 2$, the formula gives

$$a_n - 6a_{n-1} + 9a_{n-2} =$$
$$= 3^n\left[1 - \frac{2n}{3}\right] - 6\cdot 3^{n-1}\left[1 - \frac{2(n-1)}{3}\right] + 9\cdot 3^{n-2}\left[1 - \frac{2(n-2)}{3}\right]$$
$$= 3^n\left[\frac{3-2n}{3}\right] - 2\cdot 3\cdot 3^{n-1}\left[\frac{3-2(n-1)}{3}\right] + 3^2\cdot 3^{n-2}\left[\frac{3-2(n-2)}{3}\right]$$
$$= 3^n\left[\frac{3-2n}{3}\right] - 2\cdot 3^n\left[\frac{3-2(n-1)}{3}\right] + 3^n\left[\frac{3-2(n-2)}{3}\right]$$
$$= 3^{n-1}[3 - 2n] - 2\cdot 3^{n-1}[3 - 2(n-1)] + 3^{n-1}[3 - 2(n-2)]$$
$$= 3^{n-1}\left[3 - 2n - 2\cdot[3 - 2(n-1)] + 3 - 2(n-2)\right]$$
$$= 3^{n-1}[3 - 2n - 6 + 4(n-1) + 3 - 2(n-2)]$$
$$= 3^{n-1}[3 - 2n - 6 + 4n - 4 + 3 - 2n + 4] = 0$$

as required.

There is nothing that expressly precludes us from applying the results to complex roots, although we will not do so here. If $b^2 < 4c$, the two roots can be written as a complex conjugate pair

$$x_1 = \mu + i\lambda, \quad x_2 = \mu - i\lambda$$

where $\mu = -b/2$ and $\lambda = (\sqrt{4c - b^2})/2$, and a general solution takes the form

$$a_n = C_1 x_1^n + C_2 x_2^n$$

For higher degree recurrences, a consequence of the fundamental theorem of algebra is that every polynomial of degree n can be factored into a constant times factors of the form $x + a$ and $x^2 + ax + b$. Each of these give either two distinct real, one repeated real, or a pair of complex conjugate roots to the characteristic equation. Additional terms in the solution of the form r^n are produced for each distinct root, and of the form nr^n, $n^2 r^n$, for each repeated root. The general solution is the linear sum of these terms, $\sum_i C_i a_i$, where the C_i are undetermined constants.

Of particular interest to computer science is the relation between summation and recurrence. A recurrence is to a recursive function what a summation is to an iterative program, and every summation has an inherent recurrence relation embedded within it. Consider the summation

$$S_n = a_1 + a_2 + \cdots + a_n = \sum_{k=1}^{n} a_k$$

Then

$$
\begin{aligned}
S_1 &= a_1 \\
S_2 &= a_1 + a_2 = S_2 + a_2 \\
S_3 &= a_1 + a_2 + a_3 = S_2 + a_3 \\
&\vdots \\
S_n &= a_n + S_{n-1}
\end{aligned}
\tag{16.1}
$$

We can often use this concept to convert a recurrence relation to a sum. Suppose we have a general recurrence relation on r_n

$$\alpha_n r_n = \beta_n r_{n-1} + \gamma_n \tag{16.2}$$

where α_n, β_n, and γ_n are any known functions of n. The goal is to find a general solution for r_n, by converting (16.2) to a summation - like recurrence of the form

$$S_n = S_{n-1} + a_n \tag{16.3}$$

We will do this by finding a summation factor p_n such that when (16.2) is muliplied through by p_n it takes on the form (16.3). If we multiply (16.2) by p_n we have

$$p_n \alpha_n r_n = p_n \beta_n r_{n-1} + p_n \gamma_n$$

If we make the associations

$$S_n = p_n \alpha_n r_n$$
$$S_{n-1} = p_n \beta_n r_{n-1}$$
$$a_n = p_n \gamma_n$$

then we have

$$p_n \alpha_n r_n = S_n = \sum_{k=1}^{n} a_k = \sum_{k=1}^{n} p_k \gamma_k$$

and therefore an explicit solution for r_n in terms of known quantities is

$$r_n = \frac{1}{p_n \alpha_n} \sum_{k=1}^{n} p_k \gamma_k \tag{16.4}$$

The problem becomes one of finding p_n, which must work in order to satisfy $S_n = p_n \alpha_n r_n$ and $S_{n-1} = p_n \beta_n r_{n-1}$. But if $S_n = p_n \alpha_n r_n$ then we must have $S_{n-1} = p_{n-1} \alpha_{n-1} r_{n-1}$. This gives two expressions for S_{n-1}; equating them,

$$p_n \beta_n r_{n-1} = S_{n-1} = p_{n-1} \alpha_{n-1} r_{n-1}$$

The requirement simplifies to

$$p_n = p_{n-1} \frac{\alpha_{n-1}}{\beta_n}$$

Iteratively replacing p_{n-1} with its expansion for p_{n-2} on the right, and so forth, gives:

$$p_n = p_{n-q-1} \frac{\alpha_{n-1} \alpha_{n-2} \alpha_{n-3} \cdots \alpha_{n-q-1}}{\beta_n \beta_{n-1} \beta_{n-2} \cdots \beta_{n-q}} \tag{16.5}$$

There is an undetermined initial condition in the p_n, such as p_0, which we can usually set to 1, although we might pick are initial condition at some p_j, $j > 0$, especially if one of the α_k or β_k are zero for non-zero k.

In the *quicksort* algorithm, an array of times $a_1, a_2, \ldots, a_n$ is sorted as follows:

1. Pick an arbitrary element of the array, called the *pivot*.
2. Determine the location of the pivot in the sorted array by comparing it to each of the other elements in the array.
3. Place the pivot in its correct location, by exchanging places with the item there. This will divide the rest of the array into to parts. Call these RHS and LHS (right and left hand sides) of the array.
4. Sort the LHS recursively.
5. Sort the RHS recursively.

Here is a simple implementation of the quick sort in python that always chooses the first element of the array as the pivot.

```
def qsort(a):
    if len(a)<=1:
        return(a)
    pivot = a[0]
    rhs = [x for x in a[1:] if x>pivot]
    lhs = [x for x in a[1:] if x<= pivot]
    return(qsort(lhs)+[pivot]+qsort(rhs))
```

We can use the method of converting a recurrence to sum to determine the order of convergence of the quicksort algorithm.

▶▶▶ **Example 16.6.** Find a recurrence relation that gives the number of comparisons C_n required by the quicksort algorithm to sort an array of length n.

It will require $n - 1$ comparisons to determine where to place the pivot, since it must be compared with every other element of the array. If the pivot ends up at location i, the number of comparisons required to sort the LHS is C_{i-1}, and the number of comparisons required to sort the RHS is C_{n-i}.

Since the pivot might end up anywhere, we will average over all possible solutions to get the typical behavior:

$$C_n = n - 1 + \frac{1}{n} \sum_{i=1}^{n} (C_{i-1} + C_{n-i}) = n - 1 + \frac{2}{n} \sum_{i=1}^{n} C_{i-1}$$

where the final expression follows from the symmetry of the two sums. To simplify the expression, multiply through by n:

$$nC_n = n(n-1) + 2 \sum_{k=1}^{n} C_{k-1}$$

Since $C_0 = C_1 = 0$ (no comparisons are required for a length 0 or length 1 array),

$$nC_n = n(n-1) + 2\sum_{k=3}^{n} C_{k-1}$$

Shifting the index in the sum by 1 (set $j = k - 1$),

$$nC_n = n(n-1) + 2\sum_{j=2}^{n-1} C_j$$

This must also be true for $n - 1$, so

$$(n-1)C_{n-1} = (n-1)(n-2) + 2\sum_{j=2}^{n-2} C_j$$

Subtracting the last two equations gives

$$nC_n - (n-1)C_{n-1} = n(n-1) + 2\sum_{j=2}^{n-1} C_j - (n-1)(n-2) - 2\sum_{j=2}^{n-2} C_j$$
$$= n^2 - n - (n^2 - 3n + 2) + 2C_{n-1}$$
$$= 2(n-1) + 2C_{n-1}$$

Rearranging the terms, the simplified recurrence relation is

$$nC_n = (n+1)C_{n-1} + 2(n-1)$$

◀ ◀ ◀

We can solve this recurrence using the method of summation factions.

▶ ▶ ▶ **Example 16.7.** The recurrence relation for the quicksort can be expressed in the form given by (16.2) (see exercise (6)) by making the association $\alpha_n = n$, $\beta_n = n + 1$, and $\gamma_n = 2(n-1)$. Hence the general solution from (16.4) is

$$C_n = \frac{2}{np_n} \sum_{k=1}^{n} p_k(k-1)$$

where p_n is given by (16.5),

$$p_n = p_1 \frac{\alpha_{n-1}\alpha_{n-2}\cdots\alpha_1}{\beta_n\beta_{n-1}\cdots\beta_2}$$
$$= p_1 \frac{(n-1)(n-2)\cdots3\cdot2\cdot1}{(n+1)(n)(n-1)\cdots5\cdot4\cdot3}$$
$$= \frac{2}{(n)(n+1)}$$

Setting $p_1 = 1$ and plugging the formulat for p_n into the expression for C_n gives

$$C_n = \frac{2}{n} \cdot \frac{n(n+1)}{2} \sum_{k=1}^{n} \frac{2(k-1)}{k(k+1)} = 2(n+1)\left[\sum_{k=1}^{n} \frac{1}{k+1} - \sum_{k=1}^{n} \frac{1}{k(k+1)} \right]$$

The first sum is a shifted harmonic series:

$$\sum_{k=1}^{n} \frac{1}{k+1} = \frac{1}{2} + \frac{1}{3} + \cdots + \frac{1}{n+1} = -1 + H(n) + \frac{1}{n+1}$$

The second sum telescopes:

$$\begin{aligned}
\sum_{k=1}^{n} \frac{1}{k(k+1)} &= \sum_{k=1}^{n} \left[\frac{1}{k} - \frac{1}{k+1} \right] \\
&= \left[1 - \frac{1}{2} \right] + \left[\frac{1}{2} - \frac{1}{3} \right] + \cdots + \left[\frac{1}{n} - \frac{1}{n+1} \right] \\
&= 1 - \frac{1}{n+1}
\end{aligned}$$

Hence

$$\begin{aligned}
C_n &= 2(n+1)\left[-1 + H(n) + \frac{1}{n+1} - 1 + \frac{1}{n+1} \right] \\
&= 2(n+1)H(n) - 4(n+1) + 4 \\
&= 2(n+1)H(n) - 4n \qquad\qquad (16.6)
\end{aligned}$$

◀ ◀ ◀

▶ ▶ ▶ **Example 16.8.** Show that quicksort is $\Theta(n \ln n)$.

The number of comparisons is given by (16.6), $C_n = 2(n+1)H(n) - 4(n+1) + 4$.

In example 12.7, we showed that $H(n) = \Theta(\ln n)$.

The term $nH(n)$ dominates in the expression for C_n. Hence $C_n = \Theta(n \ln n)$. (Work out the details to show that C_n is both $O(n \ln n)$ and $\Omega(n \ln n)$ in exercise 8.)

Exercises

1. Explicitly calculate the first six values of the factorial sequence using the formula

$$a_0 = 1$$
$$a_n = na_{n-1} \quad \text{for } n = 1, 2, \ldots$$

and demonstrate that they correspond to $0!, 1!, \ldots, 5!$.

2. Explain why $T_0 = 0$, $T_1 = 1$, $T_2 = 3$ for the Towers of Hanoi game.

3. The recurrence relation that was found in example 1 is really an upper limit on the number of steps required for T_n.

   a) Explain why the formula found is an upper limit, i.e., the explaination given really only proves that $T_n \leqslant 2T_{n-1} + 1$.
   b) Show that it is also true that $T_n \geqslant 2T_{n-1} + 1$, thereby completing the proof of equality in the recurrence.

4. Find an explicit formula for the Fibonacci number F_n by solving the recurrence relation given in exercise 13.1.

5. Show that the if x is a root of

$$x^2 + bx + c = 0,$$

then x^n is a solution of the recurrence

$$a_n + ba_{n-1} + ca_{n-2} = 0$$

6. Show that if we make the association $\alpha_n = n$ and $\beta_n = n + 1$ then the recurrence for the quick sort

$$nC_n = (n + 1)C_{n-1} + 2(n - 1)$$

can be put into the form given by (16.2) where $\gamma_n = 2(n - 1)$.

7. Verify (16.6) by induction.

8. Work out the details of example 8.

9. Write a python program to compare the timing of quicksort and any naive sorting algorithm such as selection sort by measuring the CPU time on your computer. Run the program on arrays of various sizes, and plot the CPU as a function of array length (e.g, 10, 100, 1000, etc) on a log-log scale. What do you observe. Next, include the built-in python **sort**. How does it compare?

Ch. 16. Recurrence Relations

17. Recursion

In programming, any function that calls itself is said to be recursive. For example, we can define a naive (e.g., non-idiot-proof) implementation of the factorial function in python as

```
def fact(n):
    if n==0:
        return 1
    else:
        return n*fact(n-1)
```

Of course this function will recurse (continue to call itself forever, or at least until the stack overflows) if **n** is not an integer. This is why we called it naive.

Recursion is analagous to the priniciple of Mathematical induction, with a twist: it has a **basis** step and a **recursive** step. The basis step defines a stopping point, where computation ends (e.g., 0!) and the recursive step defines what to do for all other input. Many computer languages, such as Haskell or Scheme, implement recursion rather than iteration as their primary method of repetitive computation.

Definition 17.1. Recursive Function

We define a **recursive function** $f : \mathbb{N} \mapsto S$, where S is a any set, as follows:
- Define $f(0)$ (**basis step**)
- Define $f(n)$ in terms of $f(0), f(1), \ldots, f(n-1)$ (**recursive step**)

More generally, we do not have to start at zero in the basis. We could start at any integer a, and then define $f(n)$ in terms of $f(a)$, $f(a+1)$, ..., $f(n-1)$.

We observe that typical mathematical quantities that are normally defined iteratively as sums or products can be defined recursively. In (16.1), for example, we showed how to formulate a sum as a recurrence.

▶ ▶ ▶   **Example 17.1.**   Write the definition of the Harmonic Series

$$H_n = \sum_{k=1}^{n} \frac{1}{n} \text{ recursively.}$$

Basis Step. $H_1 = 1$.

Recursive Step. $H_n = H_{n-1} + \dfrac{1}{n}$ ◀ ◀ ◀

▶ ▶ ▶ **Example 17.2.** Write a recursive definition of $f(n) = a^n$ where $a \in \mathbb{R}$ and $n \in \mathbb{Z}^+$.

Basis Step. $f(0) = 1$

Recursive Step. $f(n) = af(n-1)$ for $n > 0$. ◀ ◀ ◀

If you are used to programming in a primarly iterative language like Python or Java, then you probably don't use recursion very much. However, many languges, such as Lisp and Haskell, use recursion almost explicitly. Operations that we would automatically implement through iteration are almost always more efficiently implemented recursively in such languages.

▶ ▶ ▶ **Example 17.3.** Write an recursive algorithm to find the largest element in a list of numbers.

Basis Step. If the length of the list is 1, return the element.

Recursive Step. Let x be the first element, and let s be the original numbers with the first element removed. Let y be the largest element in s. Return the larger of x and y ◀ ◀ ◀

A straightforward way to implement example 3 that will do this, or return **nan** if the input is an empty list, is shown in Python:

```
def recursive_max(s):
    if len(s)>1:
        return(max(s[0],recursive_max(s[1:])))
    elif len(s)==1:
        return(s[0])
    else:
        return(float("nan"))
recursive_max([5,6,9,4])
```

9

Python implements this tail recursive call in the **if** statement in the built-in function **functools.reduce**. Equivalent code using **reduce** is:

```
from functools import reduce
def rmax(s):
    if len(s)>1:
        return(reduce(max,s))
    else:
        return(float("nan"))
rmax([5,6,9,4])
```

9

Divide and Conquer Algorithms

In a **divide and conquer algorithm**, a complex problem is split up into smaller versions of the original problem. These problems can then be solved separately from one another. Since each problem is smaller, it should be considerably less difficult to solve. If an algorithm of size n requires $f(n)$ steps, and if we divide the input up into b smaller parts, then each smaller part only requires $f(n/b)$ steps to complete. Typically $f(n)$ is strictly increasing so $f(n/b)$ is smaller than $f(n)$. We may have to run our algorithm on the all the sub-problems, but in some cases, it is only necessary to only run the algorithm on one of the sub-problems. Thus in general it will be necessary to compute the smaller solution some number a times. If an additional $g(n)$ operations are also required then the total number of steps required in a divide and conquer algorithm is

$$f(n) = af(n/b) + g(n) \qquad (17.1)$$

Two popular implementations of divide and conquer algorithms are **binary search** and the **mergesort** algorithm. Binary search is used to find a particular item in a sorted array; it was even taught in elementary schools in the "old days" when there were paper dictionaries or telephone directories to find a word or name.[1] The basic idea of binary search, is to recursively divide the list or array in half. At each step, you decide if the word is in the first half or the second half. You area able to do this because you know where the split point is. For example, suppose your telephone book contains the names

---

[1] Although nobody called it binary search.

```
['Curly', 'Eric', 'George', 'John', 'Larry', 'Moe',
'Paul', 'Ringo']
```

Suppose we are looking for Moe's phone number. The first step is to split the list in half, for example, defining two new lists, **Left** and **Right**,

```
Left←['Curly', 'Eric', 'George', 'John']
Right←['Larry', 'Moe', 'Paul', 'Ringo']
```

Then we ask which list contains **'Moe'**. Since **'Moe'** ⩾ **'Larry'** (by a lexicographic comparison), we know that **'Moe'** is in **Right**. We then repeat the process recursively until we have a list with only a single element that is **'Moe'** or determine that **'Moe'** is not in the list.

Because of memory limitations it is generally more practical to pass array indices rather than entire arrays in the recursive calls. Here is one possible implementation in python, where we pass in the array and the left and right indices for searching. The function returns either the index of the key, or the value of -1 if the key is not found.

```python
def bsearch (a, l, r, x):
    if r >= l:
        m = int(l + (r - 1)/2)
        if a[m] == x:
            return m
        elif a[m] > x:
            return bsearch(a, l, m-1, x)
        else:
            return bsearch(a, m+1, r, x)
    else:
        return -1
```

If we then pass in our data as **phonebook**, we see this:

```
bsearch(phonebook, 0,7, "Moe")
```

```
5
```

Let's follow what is going on by adding an optional trace parameter.

```
def bsearch (a, l, r, x, trace=False):
    if r >= l:
        if trace: print (a[l:r+1])
        m = int(l + (r - l)/2)
        if a[m] == x:
            if trace: print (a[m], "is at index",m)
            return m
        elif a[m] > x:
            return bsearch(a, l, m-1, x, trace)
        else:
            return bsearch(a, m+1, r, x, trace)
    else:
        if trace: print(x, "is not in the dictionary")
        return -1
```

Then when we search for a key that is in the dictionary,

```
bsearch(phonebook, 0,7, "Paul", trace=True)
```

```
['Curly', 'Eric', 'George', 'John', 'Larry', 'Moe',
'Paul', 'Ringo']
['Larry', 'Moe', 'Paul', 'Ringo']
['Paul', 'Ringo']
Paul is at index 6
```

```
6
```

Next we see what happens when we search for something that is not in the dictionary:

```
bsearch(phonebook, 0,7, "Pauly", trace=True)
```

```
['Curly', 'Eric', 'George', 'John', 'Larry', 'Moe',
'Paul', 'Ringo']
['Larry', 'Moe', 'Paul', 'Ringo']
['Paul', 'Ringo']
['Ringo']
Pauly is not in the dictionary
```

```
-1
```

We can see that each recursive call is half the size of the previous call, and we only need to solve one (not both) of the smaller problems, so that in (17.1) we have $a = 1$ and $b = 2$. Since there are two decisions to be made at each step (are we done yet? and if so, which side of the list do we look at?), we have $g(n) = 2$. Thus

$$f(n) = f(n/2) + 2$$

The **mergesort** algorithm recursively sorts a list of data as follows. First, the list is recursively divided in half until only single element lists remain. A list of length one is considered sorted (by definition). Then the lists are merged into sorted lists of length 2, then length 4, then length 8, etc., until the entire list is put back together. The concept is perfectly valid even if there are not 2^k elements.

To implement a mergesort, we typically[2] need to implement two functions, a **merge** function, and a **mergesort** function. The **mergesort** function typically does the recursive subdivision, and the the **merge** typically puts the lists back together. A python implementation of **mergesort** might look like this:

```
def mergesort(a):
    if len(a)<2:
        return a
    else:
        m = len(a)//2
        LHS = mergesort(a[:m])
        RHS = mergesort(a[m:])
        return merge(LHS, RHS)
```

There is no need to sort a list of length less than 2, as these are lists of length 1, so we return the original list. If the list length is 2 or geater, we divide the list (approximately) in half and make the recursive call. In the final step, the two half lists are merged.

In python we can implement **merge** two sorted lists like this:

---

[2]Typically because it is possible to include the merge in the recursive function, but this tends to lead to less elegant code.

```
def merge(a, b):
    c=[]
    while len(a)>0 and len(b)>0:
        if a[0]<b[0]:
            c.append(a[0])
            a=a[1:]
        else:
            c.append(b[0])
            b=b[1:]
    if len(a)>0:
        c+=a
    else:
        c+=b
    return c
```

The merge sort divides the problem into two equal parts, so $b = 2$ in (17.1). Since both sub-problems are solved, we also have $a = 2$. The mergeing process requires at most $f(n) = n$ comparisons, so the recursion relation for the number of computations is

$$f(n) = 2f(n/2) + n$$

Theorem 17.1. The Master Theorem.

Suppose that a function $f : \mathbb{Z}^+ \mapsto \mathbb{R}$ is increasing, and that

$$f(n) = af(n/b) + cn^d \tag{17.2}$$

where $n = b^k, k \in \mathbb{Z}^+, a \geqslant 1 \in \mathbb{R}, b \geqslant 1 \in \mathbb{Z}, c > 0 \in \mathbb{R}$, and $d \geqslant 0 \in \mathbb{R}$, then

$$f(n) = \begin{cases} O(n^d) & \text{if } a < b^d \\ O(n^d \log_b n) & \text{if } a = b^d \\ O(n^{\log_b a}) & \text{if } a > b^d \end{cases}$$

To prove the Master Theorem we need prove the following result.

Let $n = b^k$ and suppose that

$$f(n) = af(n/b) + g(n)$$

for nonzero constants a and b and any function $g(n)$. Then

$$f(n) = f(b^k) = a^k f(1) + \sum_{j=0}^{k-1} a^j g(b_k/b_j) \qquad (17.3)$$

Proof. (Proof of theorem 17.2.) To prove the this result, observe that:

$$f(n) = af(n/b) + g(n)$$
$$f(n/b) = af(n/b^2) + g(n/b)$$
$$f(n/b^2) = af(n/b^3) + g(n/b^2)$$

$$\vdots$$

$$f(n/b^k) = af(n/b^k) + g(n/b^{k-1})$$

Substitute the second equation into the first, the the third into the second, and so on,

$$f(n) = a\big[af(n/b^2) + g(n/b)\big] + g(n)$$
$$= a\big[a\big[af(n/b^3) + g(n/b^2)\big] + g(n/b)\big] + g(n)$$

$$\vdots$$

$$= a^k f(n/b^k) + a^{k-1} g(n/b^{k-1}) + a^{k-2} g(n/b^{k-2}) + \cdots + a^0 g(n/b^0)$$

$$= a^k f(n/b^k) + \sum_{j=0}^{k-1} a^j g(n/b^j)$$

Subsitituting $n = b^k$ gives (17.3). $\quad\square$

Proof. (**Proof of the Master Theorem.**)

<u>Case 1. Let $a = b^d$.</u>

Let $f(x) = af(n/b) + cn^d$. Then from equation 17.3 with $g(n) = cn^d$

and $n = b^k$,

$$f(n) = a^k f(1) + \sum_{j=0}^{k-1} \frac{ca^j n^d}{b^{jd}}$$

$$= (b^d)^k f(1) + \sum_{j=0}^{k-1} \frac{c(b^d)^j b^{kd}}{b^j}$$

$$= (b^k)^d f(1) + \sum_{j=0}^{k-1} \frac{cb^{dj} b^{kd}}{b^{jd}} \qquad \text{cancel}$$

$$= n^d f(1) + \sum_{j=0}^{k-1} n^d \qquad \text{since } n = b^k$$

$$= n^d f(1) + ckn^d$$

Since $n = b^k$ then $\log_b n = \log_b b^k = k \log_b b = k$ and therefore for sufficiently large n

$$f(n) = n^d f(1) + cn^d \log_b n$$
$$\leqslant n^d f(1) \log_b n + cn^d \log_b n$$
$$= (c + f(1))n^d \log_b n$$

Thust $f(n) = O(n^d \log_b n)$.

Cases 2. Suppose $a \neq b^d$. Using $n = b^k$,

$$f(n) = a^k f(1) + \sum_{j=0}^{k-1} \frac{ca^j b^{kd}}{b^{jd}}$$

$$= a^k f(1) + b^{kd} c \sum_{j=0}^{k-1} \left(\frac{a}{b^d}\right)^j \qquad \text{geometric series}$$

$$= a^k f(1) + cn^d \frac{(a/b^d)^k - 1}{(a/b^d) - 1}$$

$$= a^k f(1) + cn^d \frac{a^k/n^d - 1}{a/b^d - 1}$$

where the last step uses $b^k = n$. Hence

$$f(n) = a^k f(1) + c\frac{a^k - n^d}{a/b^d - b^d/b^d}$$

$$= a^k f(1) + \frac{cb^d}{a - b^d}a^k - \frac{cb^d n^d}{a - b^d} = C_1 n^d + C_2 a^k$$

where $C_1 = b^d c/(b^d - a)$ and $C_2 = f(1) + \dfrac{cb^d}{a - b^d}$ are constants.

Case 2a. $a < b^d$. Start with $f(n) = C_1 n^d + C_2 a^k$.

Since $a < b^d$ then

$$\begin{aligned}
f(n) &= C_1 n^d + C_2 a^k \\
&< C_1 n^d + C_2 b^{dk} \\
&= C_1 n^d + C_2 n^d &&\text{because } n = b^k \\
&= (C_1 + C_2)n^d
\end{aligned}$$

Hence $f = O(n^d)$.

Case 2b. $a > b^d$. Since $n = b^k$ then $\log_b n = k$, and therefore

$$\begin{aligned}
f(n) &= C_1 n^d + C_2 a^k \\
&= C_1 (b^k)^d + C_2 a^{\log_b n} \\
&= C_1 (b^d)^k + C_2 a^{\log_b n} \\
&< C_1 a^k + C_2 a^{\log_b n} &&\text{since } b^d < a \\
&= C_1 a^{\log_b n} + C_2 a^{\log_b n} &&\text{since } k = \log_b n \\
&= (C_1 + C_2)a^{\log_b n}
\end{aligned}$$

Recall that for any x, y (positive) and for any positive base logarithm,

$$\begin{aligned}
(\log a) \log b &= (\log b) \log a \\
\log\left[b^{\log a}\right] &= \log\left[a^{\log b}\right]
\end{aligned}$$

Therefore

$$a^{\log_b n} = n^{\log_b a}$$

As a result

$$f(n) = (C_1 + C_2)n^{\log_b a}$$

and therefore f is $O(n^{\log_b a})$ as required. This completes the proof of the master theorem.

$\square$

▶ ▶ ▶ **Example 17.4.** Use the master theorem to estimate a bounds on the number of computations for the binary search.

Since $f(n) = f(n/2) + 2$, we have $a = 1$, $b = 2$, $c = 2$ and $d = 0$ in (17.2). Hence $a = 1 = 2^0 = b^d$ and therefore

$$f(n) = O(n^d \log_b n) = O(n^0 \log_2 n) = O(\log_2 n)$$

◀ ◀ ◀

▶ ▶ ▶ **Example 17.5.** Use the master theorem to estimate a bounds on the number of computations for the mergesort algorithm.

Since $f(n) = 2f(n/2) + n$, a comparison with (17.2) gives $a = 2$, $b = 2$, $c = 1$, and $d = 1$. Hence $a = 2 = 2^1 = b^d$. Therefore $f(n) = O(n^d \log_b n) = O(n \log_2 n)$ ◀ ◀ ◀

Exercises

1. Define a recursive function that will add the sum of of the numbers in a finite sequence.

2. Implement a recursive function in Python that will sum of the numbers in a finite array.

3. Implement a recursive function for a^n in Python.

4. Write a recursive implementation of the harmonic function (example 1) in Python.

5. Write a recursive implementation of the factorial function in Python using **reduce**.

6. The Ackerman function is defined recursively on pairs of the positive integers as follows:

$$A_{0,n} = n + 1, \forall n \geqslant 0$$
$$A_{m,0} = A_{m-1,1}, \forall m > 0$$
$$A_{m,n} = A_{m-1,A_{m,n-1}}, \forall m, n > 0$$

Calculate $A_{1,2}$ carefully showing each step of your calculation.

7. Write a recursive Python function **A(m,n)** to calculate the Ackerman function defined in exercise 6. Print a table of values of $A_{m,n}$ for $0 \leqslant m \leqslant 3$ and $0 \leqslant n \leqslant 4$. Note: it is not recommended to use this method for larger indices. The Ackerman functions grows rapidly. For example, $A_{4,3} = 2^{2^{65536}} - 3$.

18 . Languages and Regular Expressions

Regular expressions are used in many different computer languages for pattern matching. They were first invented by Stephen Kleene (1909-1994) in 1951 to describe the collection of strings that are in a computer language. Here we provide an introduction to the concept as it provides us examples of recursive set definitions.

Kleene's was to describe **languages**, and (written) are based on **alphabets**. Alphabets are collections of symbols. You can think of the symbols as single characters on your keyboard such as **'d'** or **'&'**. We will often omit the quotes around the characters except when we want to be absolutely clear where the character begins or ends; this will be more important when we are writing out strings, which are sequences of characters. Sometimes we will refer to the characters as **letters**, although this term can be misleading, especially if non-alphabetic characters are included in the alphabet.

Definition 18.1. Alphabet

An **alphabet** Σ is any set of characters.

The alphabet in python contains upper case latin letters, lower case letters, digits, and the underscore character. In python we distinguish between upper case and lower case letters, so that the letters **P** and **p** are different.

Strings are finite sequences of characters.

Definition 18.2. String

Let Σ be any alphabet. Then a **string over** Σ is any finite sequence of characters chosen from Σ, or the null string, denoted by ϵ.

Generally we will write strings by writing the characters right next to one another, and will omit any delimiting quotes unless they are absolutely necessary to identify the end of the string.

A python string is drawn from its alphabet but may not start with a digit. We generally write down python strings by enclosing them in single or double quotes, such as 'HELLO'. The null string is denoted in python by a pair of repeated quotes.

▶ ▶ ▶ **Example 18.1.** Suppose $\Sigma = \{\mathbf{a}, \mathbf{b}, \mathbf{d}\}$. Then examples of strings over Σ are **a**, **ab**, **bad**, **abbbbaaabbbadd**, and ϵ. ◀ ◀ ◀

Definition 18.3. String Length

The **length of a string** is the number of characters in the string. The length of the null string is zero.

▶ ▶ ▶ **Example 18.2.** Let $\Sigma = \{\mathbf{a}, \mathbf{b}, \mathbf{d}\}$. Then the length of **a** is 1; the length of **ab** is 2; the length of **bad** is 3; and the length of **abbbbaaabbbadd** is 14. ◀ ◀ ◀

In python, the length of a string is given by the **len** function.

```
print(len("helloworld"))
```

10

A **formal language over** Σ is then any set of strings defined over Σ, i.e., a specific collection of strings constructed from that alphabet. We will be interested in several specific formal languages.

Definition 18.4. Formal Language

Let Σ be an alphabet. Then a **formal language** L over Σ is any set of of strings over Σ. In particular,
- Σ^n = the set of all strings of length n defined over Σ.
- Σ^+ = the set of all strings of length greater than one defined over Σ.
- Σ^* = the set of all strings defined over Σ. (Kleene Closure of Σ)

We can build up new strings from older strings by a process called **concatenation**. When we concatenate two strings together, we write down the sequence of characters in the first string followed by the sequence of

---

characters in the second string. For example, if **x** and **y** are strings over Σ such that **x=abc** and **y=pqr** then the concatenation of **x** and **y** is **abcpqr**.

Sometimes it is convenient to use an operator such as a small dot for concatenation:

$$\textbf{abc·pqr} \rightarrow \textbf{abcpqr}$$

Here we have introduced the **production arrow** notation, which means the operation between the strings on left hand side of the expression produces a new string on the right hand side of the expression.

We can also concatenate languages. Suppose that L and L' are languages over an alphabet Σ. Then the concatenation of L and L', denoted by LL', is the language

$$LL' = \{\ell\ell' | \ell \in L \wedge \ell' \in L'\}$$

▶ ▶ ▶ **Example 18.3.** Let Σ be the set of digits **0** through **9**.

Let L be the language over Σ consisting of the set of all 3-digit sequences that do not contain either a **0** or **1** as the first digit.

Let L' be the langauge over Σ consisting of all 7-digit sequences that do not contain either a **0** or **1** as the first digit.

Then LL' consists of the set of all valid phone numbers in the North American phone numbering asignment of 1947. ◀ ◀ ◀

We want to be able to easily describe the patterns of digits in languages such as the North American phone numbering plan, as well as much more complex patterns, up to and including computer languages. We will describe rules to do this recursively.

Regular Expressions

The set of **regular expressions** over an alphabet σ, denoted by $R(\sigma)$ is defined recursively as follows:

Basis: a) $\emptyset \in R(\Sigma)$ (emptyset is recognized)
             b) $\epsilon \in R(\Sigma)$ (null strings are recognized)

c) $(\forall a \in \Sigma)(a \in R(\Sigma)$ (all letters in the alphabet)

Recursive: Let $r, s \in R(\Sigma)$. Then (assuming that "(", ")", "—" and "*" are not in Σ)[1] we can extend $R(\Sigma)$ with each of the following:

    a) (rs) (concatentation) - e.g., if **fred** and **smith** are in $R(\Sigma)$, then so is **fredsmith**.

    b) $(r|s)$ (choice operator) - e.g, if **(fred|smith)** matches both **fred** and **smith**.

    c) (r^*) (Kleene closure of r) - **(01)** * matches $\{\epsilon, \mathbf{01}, \mathbf{0101}, \mathbf{010101}, \ldots\}$

▶ ▶ ▶   **Example 18.4.** Let $\Sigma = \{\mathbf{a}, \mathbf{b}, \mathbf{c}\}$.

Then the regular expression **a | ((b | c) *)** matches (among other strings):

$$\{\mathbf{a}, \mathbf{b}, \mathbf{c}, \mathbf{bc}, \mathbf{bbbcbc}, \ldots\}$$

◀ ◀ ◀

Within a regular expression we are allowed to use parenthesis to specify the order of precedence. The order of precedence is as follows:

1. As specified by parenthesis
2. Kleene Closure (* operator)
3. Concentention
4. Choice (vertical line operator)

Regular expressions cna be used to define any computer language. We use the notation $L : A \longrightarrow B$ to indicate that $L(a)$ is a mapping that produces elements of the language B (set of strings) from the string $a \in A$.

Definition 18.5. Language Defined by Regular Expression

The language defined by a regular expression r over Σ is defined recursively as follows:
    Basis :

        a) $L(\varnothing) \longrightarrow \varnothing$
        b) $L(\epsilon) \longrightarrow \{\epsilon\}$

---

[1]If they are, we replace the them with other symbols that are not in Σ.

c) For all $a \in \Sigma$, $L(a) \longrightarrow \{a\}$

Recursion : Let $L(r)$ and $L(r')$ be the languages defined by the regular expressions r and r' over Σ. Then we can also add

a) $L(rr') \longrightarrow L(r)L(r')$

b) $L(r|r') \longrightarrow L(r) \cup L(r')$

c) $L(r*) \longrightarrow (L(r))^*$

▶ ▶ ▶ **Example 18.5.** Write a regular expression that will match all strings of alternating zeros and ones that hvae even length.

Let $\Sigma = \{0, 1\}$. Then one possible solution is $r = (10)*|(01)*$. ◀ ◀ ◀

▶ ▶ ▶ **Example 18.6.** A string over $\Sigma = \{0, 1\}$ is said to have **even parity** of it contains an even number of ones. Find a regular expression that matches all strings with even parity over $\Sigma = \{0, 1\}$.

One possible solution is **(0 | (10*1))***. ◀ ◀ ◀

▶ ▶ ▶ **Example 18.7.** Find a regular expression that matches a string of ones and zeros that notes not have any consecutive ones.

To construct the expression, we note that if there is a 1 any place except the last digit, it must be followed by a zero. To handle the "what if it ends in a one" we give an optional ending term of either 1 or ϵ. Then whatever precedes this should end in a zero:

$$(\text{something}) \, (\epsilon \,|\, 1)$$

Our "something" can be either zero, or something without any repeated ones:

$$(0 \,|\, \text{something with repeated 1's}) \, (\epsilon \,|\, 1)$$

To prevent repeated ones, we declared earlier that a one must be always followed by a zero.

$$(0 \,|\, 10) \, (\epsilon \,|\, 1)$$

Then the entire first part can be repeated one or more times:

$$(0 \,|\, 10)^* \, (\epsilon \,|\, 1)$$

◀ ◀ ◀

We note in passing that regular expressions are not unique! It is often possible to find many different solutions to the same problem. Consider, for example, the set of strings defined by $(0|1)^*$ and $(0^*|1^*)^*$.

A number of computer languages include shorthands that expedite the process of writing regular expressions. Note that these are not standard regular expression syntax but are fairly common throughout the industry.

Table 18.1. Sample Shorthand Expressions Used in Regular Expressions

[A-C]	equivalent to **(A|B|C)**
[0-9]	equivalent to **(0|1|2|3|4|5|6|7|8|9)**
.	matches any single character
A.C	matches **AxC** where **x** is any letter in Σ.
r$^+$	equivalent to **rr***
[A-Z]$^+$	is an non-empty string of upper-case letters.
r?	is equivlent to **(|ϵr)**.
r{n}	means precisely n repeats

Backus-Naur Form (BNF)

A higher level syntax than normal forms is generally used to specify computer languages. The Python web pages, for example, generally give a detailed specification of all commands in **Backus-Naur Form.**[2] Much like regular expressions, BNF is a **metasyntax**, i.e., a syntax used to describe the syntax of another language. BNF works for a certain class of languages that have what are called **context-free grammars** (so you can't use it to describe most natural languages, which are not context-free).

BNF is describes the syntax of expressions by **terminals** and **non-terminals**. In standard BNF, the syntax is

```
<symbol> ::= expression
```

where **<symbol>** is a nonterminal, and **expression** is a terminal. In BNF, anything inside of **< >** symbols is a description or a name of what goes there, while anything else is literally replaced by the text you see written there. Square brackets are used to enclose optional parts of the expression,

---

[2]BNF is named for John Backus who developed it in 1959, and Peter Naur who created his own version of BNF, naming the original Backus Normal Form in 1963. Donald Knuth (who has the final word in everything) decided that it must be called Backus-Naur form in 1964 and the name has stuck.

and alternate choices are separated by vertical lines. Curly brackets are used for precedence of evaluation. An example is

```
<fullname>    ::= <first-name> [<middle-name>] <last-name>
<first-name> ::= <name>
<middle-name>::= <name>
<last-name>   ::= <name>
<name>        ::= <upper-case-letter>{<lower-case-letter>}+
```

The **+** and ***** are used in the same manner as in regular expressions. The plus sign **+** on line 5 means that **one or more instance** of a lower-case-letter is required. In some cases there may be something that occurs **zero or more times**, which is specified with an asterisk *****.

This would have to be followed by specifications both for **<upper-case-letter>** and also for **<lower-case-letter>**, e.g.,

```
<upper-case-letter> := "A"|"B"|"C"|"D"| ... |"Z"
<lower-case-letter> := "a"|"b"|"c"|"d"| ... |"z"
```

The triple dots used here are for illustration only; you actually have to include every letter in the character set for a correct specification. The above 7 lines of BNF, taken together, give a BNF specification of names composed of first and last names, that may include an optional middle name. The specification fails for people who only have one name, or who have more than one middle or last names. Such language specifications are often used by language parsing programs to read data into forms, for example, so that programmers do not have to do syntax checksing themselves. They just write the BNF.

Syntactically there is no reason for distinguishing between the three types of names on the first four lines, so this specification would more likely be written as

```
<fullname>    ::= <name> [<name>] <name>
<name> ::= <upper-case-letter>{<lower-case-letter>}+
<upper-case-letter> := "A"|"B"|"C"|"D"| ... |"Z"
<lower-case-letter> := "a"|"b"|"c"|"d"| ... |"z"
```

The Python specification omits the symbols **< >** from the non-terminals, and replaces the curly brackets **{ }** with square brackets **[ ]**. It also omits the double dots vertical lines in the alphabet specifications. The equivalent specification in the modified BNF-like format would be

```
fullname   ::= name [name] name
name   ::= upper-case-letter [lower-case-letter]+
upper-case-letter := "A"..."Z"
lower-case-letter := "a"..."z"
```

Exercises

1. Write down at least 5 patterns that each of the following regular expresions match.

   a) **(01*)|((1*)0)**
   b) **(01)*|((1*)0)**
   c) **(01)|((1*)0)**
   d) **10*1110**

2. Write a regular expression to match a hyphenated US social security number.

3. Look up the linux **grep** command. It has an extensive library for pattern matching against the contents of files and can be run from the command line. Find all the files on your computer that contain a string that begins with **ba** and ends with nas (e.g, it should find all the files that have words like bananas or cabanas, in it.

4. Write a regular expression to match any integer.

5. Write a BNF specification for a floating point expresion (e.g., 1.5432E-17; the sign and the exponent are optional in the expression.)

6. Write a BNF specifcation for an integer assignment statement that allows parenthesis, multiplication, addition, subtraction, and division operators. You may assume that **integer** and **identifiers** have already been defined.

19. Graph Theory

Graphs are often used to describe relationships between objects. The vertices could represent objects such as locations (islands, cities, airports) on a map; molecules in a metabolic network; or levels of educational attainment. The corresponding relations might then be, for example, pathways between locations on a road map; the phosphorylation pathways in a metabolic network; or the process of stepping through the levels of educational advancement. Mathematically, we denote a **graph** by two things:

- a set **v** of **vertices**, such as the cities on the road map; and
- a set **e** of **edges**, such as the roads between the cities.

We denote the graph by $g(v, e)$.

Definition 19.1. Graph

A graph $g(v, e)$ is a set v, consisting of one or more vertices, taken together with a set of zero or more edges e, where each element of e is a set consisisting of a pair of elements in v.

We label the vertices (sometimes called **nodes**) and the edges by either sets of length 2, as in

$$g = \{\overbrace{\{a, b, c, d\}}^{V}, \overbrace{\{\{a, b\}, \{b, c\}, \{b, d\}, \{c, d\}\}}^{E}\}$$

or ordered pairs, as in

$$h = \{\{a, b, c, d\}, \{(a, b), (b, c), (b, d), (c, d)\}\}$$

In the later case the graph is said to be **directed graph**. In a directed graph, we treat the edges like one-way streets: there pointfrom a to b, from b to c, from b to d and from c to d like one way streets. You cannot move in the other direction along these edges. Directed graphs are sometimes called **digraphs**. A directed graph may have more than edge conecting the same two vertices (think of two different roads connecting the same two

Figure 19.1.: Illustration of simple graph (left) and simple directed graph (right).

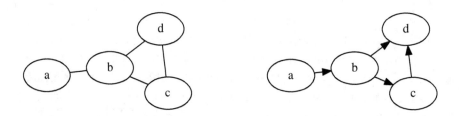

cities; see figure 19.2). Because we allow for repetation, the collection of edges in a directed graph is a multiset, not a set. A **multiset** has the same properties as a set, but we allow (and keep), repeated copies of otherwise identical objects.

Figure 19.2.: A directed graph $\{\{a, b, c, d\}, \{(a, b), (b, c), (c, b), (b, d), (d, d), (d, e), (d, e)\}\}$.

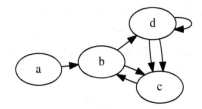

Definition 19.2. Directed Graph

A **directed graph** $g(v, e)$ is a set v, consisting of one or more vertices, taken together with a multiset of one or more edges e, where each element of e is an ordered pair of elements in v.

Since each edge consists of two vertices, these two vertices are sometimes called the **end points** of the edge. It is important to remember, however, that there is not necessarily any inherent geometry associated with the graph. Two vertices are said to be **adjacent** if they share an edge. Again stealing some vocabulary from geometry, if any vertex i is part of any edge $p = \{i, j\}$ or any directed edge $q = (i, j)$, we say that i is **incident** on p (or q). The number (count) of edges that are incident on any perticular vertex is called the **degree** of that vertex. In figure 19.1, for example, vertices a, b, c and d have degrees 1, 3, 2 and 2, respectively. The degree of a graph is the sum of the degrees of all the vertices in the graph. (Any loop from one vertex to itself is counted twice in the calculation of the degree of a vertex.) We use the notation $\deg(v)$ and $\deg(g)$ to denote the degree of a vertex and the degree of a graph, respectively.

Theorem 19.1. Handshake Theorem

Let $g(v, e)$ be a graph with $V > 1$ vertices and $E > 0$ edges. Then

$$\deg(g) = 2E$$

and in particular, the degree of a graph is always even.

Proof. Denote the vertices by $v_1, v_2, \ldots$, and let e_{ij} denote the edge connecting vertices v_i and v_j. Then e_{ij} contributes 1 to $\deg(v_i)$ and 1 to $\deg(v_j)$. Hence each edge contributes a factor of 2 to $\deg(g)$, and $\deg(g)=2E$. Since E is an integer and $2|2E$, we conclude that $\deg(g)$ is even. $\square$

Theorem 19.2. Even/Odd Theorem

Every graph has an even number of vertices with an odd degree.

Proof. Let g be a graph.

1. By the Handshake theorem theorem $\deg(g)$ is even. Hence there is some integer k such that $\deg(g) = 2k$.
2. Let n_{even} be the number of vertices with even degree.
3. Since every even vertex has an even number vertices, there is

---

some integer m such that $n_{even} = 2m$.

4. Let n_{odd} be the number of vertices with odd degree.
5. The total number of vertices is the sum of the number vertices with even degree and the number of vertices with odd degree,

$$\deg(g) = n_{\text{even}} + n_{\text{odd}}$$

6. By substitution, $2k = n_{\text{odd}} + 2m$
7. By rearranging, $n_{\text{odd}} = 2(k - m)$. Hence $2 | n_{\text{odd}}$

The last step proves that there are an even number of vertices with odd degree. □

Graph Representations

One of representing the graph is with its **connection matrix** M. Enumerate the nodes by a list starting with 1; for example, in figures 19.1 and 19.2 we can enumerate the sequence of nodes $\{a, b, c, d\}$ as $\{1, 2, 3, 4\}$. Then we set $M_{ij} = 1$ if the two nodes are connected, and $M_{ij} = 0$ if they are not connected. The connection matrix for a non-directed graph is always symmetric. For the left-hand graph of figure 19.1,

$$M = \begin{bmatrix} 0 & 1 & 0 & 0 \\ 1 & 0 & 1 & 1 \\ 0 & 1 & 0 & 1 \\ 0 & 1 & 1 & 0 \end{bmatrix}$$

When the graph is directed, then M_{ij} gives the number of arrows emanating from node i to node j. For the graph in figure 19.2, we have

$$M = \begin{bmatrix} 0 & 1 & 0 & 0 \\ 0 & 0 & 1 & 1 \\ 0 & 1 & 0 & 0 \\ 0 & 0 & 2 & 1 \end{bmatrix}$$

A connection matrix is easy to implement computationally. However, most graphs will be sparsely connected. For example, suppose $F(v, e)$ is a graph that represents the collection of all people who use Facebook. Each vertex is a Facebook user. In early 2018, there were approximately 2×10^9 (two billion) Facebook users. A connection matrix would require over 10^{18} words of storage - more than an exabyte. But the average facebook user has around 300 friends, so fewer than 10^{12} entries in the matrix will be non-zero. In other words, only around one out of every million entries in the connection matrix is non-zero. It is far more space efficient to store a list of connections corresponding to each edge.

Returning to the graph in figure 19.3, there are several ways we could store this in Python.

- Using a connection list:

```
v = [1,2,3,4,5,6,7]
e = [[1,4],[1,5],[2,4],[2,5],[2,6],[3,5],[3,6],[3,7]]
g = (v,e)
```

  With a connection list, we access everything using indices. The problem with this type of data structure is that if we want to inquire about which edges emanate from a particular vertex, we have to search through the entire list. We can do this for cheap in Python with the **filter** function. When you execute **filter(f,u)** on a list **u** it returns every element of **u** for which **f(u)** returns **True**. For example, to find all the edges that have vertex 2 in them,

```
list(filter(lambda x:2 in x, e))
```

```
[[2, 4], [2, 5], [2, 6]]
```

  The **lambda** function was a quick way to define an unnamed function that that returns **True** if 2 is in a list and **False** otherwise. It is completely equivalent to writing

```
def f(x):
        return (2 in x)
list(filter(f, e))
```

- Using a connection dictionary:

```
g={1:[4,5],
   2:[4,5,6],
   3:[5,6,7]}
```

- As a class. You could use either a list or a dictionary (or some other organization) to store the data, and then add methods to add and remove edges, locate nodes and edges, and do whatever sort of analysis you might find useful. For example, **graphviz**-based visualization packages such as the one discussed below store the graph information as a class and use various methods to modify the layout and other visualization information.

Special Types of Graphs

If one graph is completely contained in another graph, then we say that it is a subgraph.

Definition 19.3. Subgraph

We say that $h(v, e)$ is a subgraph of $g(v', e')$ if $v \subseteq v'$ and $e \subseteq e'$.

▶ ▶ ▶ **Example 19.1.** The graph $p = \{\{c, d\}, \{(d, c), (d, c), (d, d)\}\}$ is a subgraph of the graph shown in figure 19.2.

Furthermore, the graph $q = \{\{b, c, d\}, \{(b, d), (b, c), (c, b), (d, c), (d, c), (d, d)\}\}$ is also a subgraph of the graph shown in figure 19.2. Furthermore, p is a subgraph of q. ◀ ◀ ◀

In a **bipartite graph**, the vertices can be partitioned into two subsets such that every edge in the original graph has one endpoint in each subset. In the graph illustrated in figure 19.3, each of the nodes on the top is connected only to a node on the bottom layer. There are not any connections within the top layer, and there are not any connections within the bottom layer.

Definition 19.4. Partition

A **partition** of a set S is a decomposition into subsets $S_1, S_2, \ldots, S_n$ such that (a) $S_i \cap S_j = \varnothing$ for all $i \neq j$; and (b) $S = S_1 \cup S_2 \cdots \cup S_n$.

Figure 19.3.: A bipartite graph.

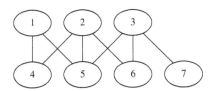

Definition 19.5. Bipartite Graph

Let $g(v, e)$ be a graph. If there is a partition of v into two subsets v_1 and v_2 such that for every edge $\{i, j\} \in e$ either (a) $i \in v_1$ and $j \in v_2$; or (b) $i \in v_2$ and $j \in v_1$.

In a **complete graph**, every node is connected to every other node in the graph. Figure 19.4 shows a complete graph with 5 vertices and 10 edges. In general, the total number of edges E a complete graph is

$$E = \binom{v}{2} = \frac{v!}{2(v-2)!} = \frac{v(v-1)}{2}$$

Most of the time, it is easier for humans to understand the picture of a graph if the lines do not intersect. Sometimes can redraw a graph with intersecting lines so that do not intersect. Graphs with lines that do not intersect are called planar graphs. Not all graphs can be turned into planar graphs. Examples include the complete graph with 5 vertices.

Definition 19.6. Planar Graph

A planar graph is a graph that can be drawn without any intersecting edges.

The regions that can be colored (filled in) between the edges of a planar graph are called **faces**. There is an entire literature devoted to **graph coloring**. For example, given any particular planar graph, how many colors does it take color it to ensure that no two adjacent faces are filled in with the same color?

Figure 19.4.: A copmlete graph with 5 vertices.

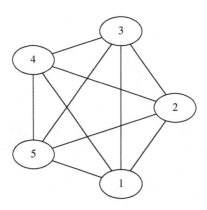

A **tree** is a graph without circuits. A circuit is any path in graph that starts and stops at the same vertex without passing over the same edge twice. Trees are often used to represent hierarchical relationships (such as families) and decision processes (such as which course to take). trees are often used to parse expressions when writing computer programs (AST, Abstract Syntax Tree) (figure 19.5). One particular node in the tree is designated as the **root**. Vertices that have degree 1 are called **leaves**. A tree that contains only degree 1 (leaves) or degree 2 nodes is called a **binary tree**. Each node in a binary tree may have two **daughters**, which are sometimes called **siblings**, and one **parent** or **mother** node. The leaves have no daughters, and the root has no parent. The **height** of a tree is the maximum number of nodes that must be traversed to reach any leaf from the root node.

In some applications it is useful to designate the two daughters as **left** and **right**; this is also helpful in writing class definitions. For example if a binary operation is represented by a parent node for exponentiation, then the operation x^y (with left daughter x and right daughter y) needs to be distinguished from the operation y^x (with left daughter y and right daughter x).

Trees are easier to represent than graphs because the structure is better

Figure 19.5.: Illustration of a syntax tree for the expression $-b + \sqrt{b^2 - 4ac}$.

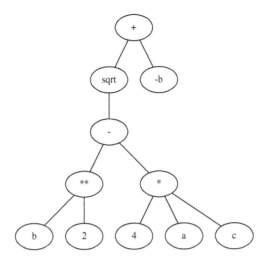

determine. The general idea is to define a basic class that contains a place to put data and a place to point to both the left and the right subtrees. Here is an **init** method for this type of class definition:

```
class Tree:
    def __init__(self, data, left=None, right=None):
        self.data = data
        self.left  = left
        self.right = right
```

You could write additional methods to search, print, or perform other operations on this kind of tree. If you will need to change the pointers you will need, for example, some sort of **set_left_subtree** and a **set_right_subtree** methods. A separate **add** or **add_node** class is not really needed, since you can build up the tree as a linked list by defining the pointers at creation.

Plotting Graphs

It is useful to display the graph with a picture (see figure 19.1) *but there is nothing inherent in the definition of a graph that requires a picture.* These graphs are easy to illustrate in Python using Graphviz. Graphviz is actually a graphing visualization and layout application that we can access in Python via any of several wrappers. One such wrapper is **pygraphviz**. We can draw the graphs g and h defined above using **pygraphviz** with the following code.

```
import pygraphviz as pgv

G=pgv.AGraph()
G.add_node("a")
G.add_node("b")
G.add_node("c")
G.add_node("d")
G.add_edge("a","b")
G.add_edge("b","c")
G.add_edge("b","d")
G.add_edge("c","d")
G.layout()
G.draw("the-undirected-graph.pdf")

H=pgv.AGraph(directed=True)
H.add_node("a")
H.add_node("b")
H.add_node("c")
H.add_node("d")
H.add_edge("a","b")
H.add_edge("b","c")
H.add_edge("b","d")
H.add_edge("c","d")
H.layout()
H.draw("the-directed.graph.pdf")
```

The above code was used to produce the two images illustrated in figure 19.1. Graph images are written to files and can be viewed separately. The variables **G** or **H** in the code actually contain **Graphviz** code. If you have graphviz rendering software, you could save this code with is your file has an extension **.dot** in the call to the **draw** method. The **dot** code looks something like this:

```
strict digraph {
    graph [bb="-113.02,-47.794,80.879,59.55"];
    node [label="\N"];
    a    [height=0.5,pos="-86.018,-10.101", width=0.75];
    b    [height=0.5, pos="-13.203,-1.6554", width=0.75];
    a -> b [pos="e,-39.9,-4.7518 -59.318,-7.004 -56.251,
        -6.6483 -53.085,-6.2811 -49.916,-5.9135"];
    c    [height=0.5, pos="53.879,-29.794", width=0.75];
```

```
    b -> c [pos="e,30.978,-20.188 9.8827,-11.339 13.613,
        -12.904 17.536,-14.549 21.438,-16.186"];
    d   [height=0.5, pos="45.343,41.55",width=0.75];
    b -> d  [pos="e,26.949,27.976 5.0003,11.778 9.364,
        14.999 14.113,18.503 18.769,21.94"];
    c -> d  [pos="e,47.526,23.305 51.725,-11.791 50.822,
        -4.2445 49.75,4.7134 48.745,13.113"];
}
```

Isomporphism versus Equality

Consider the following three graphs:

$$g = \{\{p, q, r, s\}, \{\{p, q\}, \{q, r\}, \{r, s\}, \{s, p\}\}\}$$
$$h = \{\{p, q, r, s\}, \{\{p, q\}, \{q, r\}, \{r, s\}, \{s, p\}\}\}$$
$$i = \{\{a, b, c, d\}, \{\{a, b\}, \{b, c\}, \{c, d\}, \{d, a\}\}\}$$

Graphs g and h are equal, because every vertex is identical and every edge is identical. Graphs i was generated from g by a simple renaming: p to a, q to b, r to c, and s to d. The graphs are almost identical but they are not equal. They share a property known as isomorphism. These graphs could represent the routes that three different pilots take every day when flying their planes. Vertices p, q, r and s might represent Los Angeles, San Francisco, Seattle, and San Diego, while vertices a, b, c and d could represent Paris, London, Manchester, and Edinburgh. All three pilots fly a loop three four cities, but the first two pilots fly through the same four cities.

If two sets have the same structure, we say that they are **isomorphic**. An **isomorphism** is a one to one relationship between sets (see definition 12.3). The collection of all sets that are isomorphic to one another is called an **equivalence class**. Graphs are like polygons without distances and angle measures. Only the connectivity between the vertices is important. So if we are interested in comparing two graphs, we will use the concept of isomporphism.

An isomporphism between two graphs g and h is a bijection $\varphi : V(g) \mapsto V(h)$ between the vertices of g and the vertices of h such that if $\{a, b\}$ is an edge in g then $\{\varphi(a), \varphi(b)\}$ is an edge in h. Since ϕ is a bijection, this

---

definition works both ways: if $\{p, q\}$ is any edge in h then $\{\varphi^{-1}(p), \varphi^{-1}(q)\}$ is an edge of g.

Consider polygons. All triangles are isomorphic to one another, in the sense that we can define a bijection between the vertices of the first triangle and the second, and we can define a bijection between the edges of the first triangle and the second. However, no triangle is isomorphic to any quadrilaterial, and no quadrilaterial is isomorphic to any hexadecagon. Similarly all quadrilaterals are isomorphic, as we can define an isomorphism between any two of them. So we can define equivalence classes among the polygons. As we know, the equivalence class of triangles contains many differnt types of triangles, such as the 30-60-90 and the 45-45-90 triangle. Thus if $\triangle ABC$ is 30-60-90 and $\triangle DEF$ is 45-45-90, the two triangles are clearly not equal to one another. But they share the same topology: three vertices, and three edges.

Euler and Hamilton Paths

Definition 19.7. Path

Let $g(v, e)$ be a graph with vertices v and edges e. Then a **path** through g is a sequence of adjacent vertices.

Is there an easy way to walk through a large museum with many connecting room in such a way that we can visit every every room once without going through any door twice? If we represent the rooms by vertices and the doors between rooms as edges, then the answer to this question is called an Euler Path. If there are rooms with only one door then of course we will not be able to do this, as we will have to go out through the door we came in. But most museums are designed to optimize traffic flow, so in many cases there is an Euler path.

Definition 19.8. Euler Path

Let $g(v, e)$ be a graph with vertices v and edges e. The an **Euler Path** is a sequence of vertices that traverses each edge precisely once. If the Euler Path starts and stops at the same vertex it is called an **Euler Circuit**.

Note that we are allowed to pass through the same room of the museum multiple times, we just can't enter or leave it through the same door if we are following an Euler path.

Theorem 19.3. Euler Circuit Theorem

There is an Euler circuit through a graph if and only if every vertex has an even degree.

The contrapositive of the Euler Circuit Theorem rules out circuits through museums that have rooms with single doors. It also rules out circuit through museums that rooms with three doors, and this might not have been so obvious. See figure 19.6; there is no Euler circuit through this floor plan because four of the rooms have an odd number of doors. Iff we close some of the doors, such as we have done in figure 19.7, there is an Euler circuit, such as $\{1, 2, 3, 4, 1, 5, 6, 7, 1\}$.

The Euler circuit requires us to visit every edge precisely once, but we are allowed to pass through the same vertex more than once. In the museum, we could only use each door once but could pass through a room more than once. In the Euler circuit we passed through room 1 more than once, for example. If we want to visit every vertex precisely once, rather than every edge precisely once, we need to find a Hamiltonian path. A Hamiltonian circuit, on the other hand, would take us through every room precisely once. There is no Hamiltonian circuit for the museum floor plans in figures 19.6 and 19.7 because you must pass through room 1 more than once on any path that visits all the rooms.

Figure 19.6.: Left: Floor plan of a museum. There is no Euler circuit for this floor plan, because rooms 2, 3, 6 and 7 each have an odd number of doors. Right: Graph representation of the floor plan.

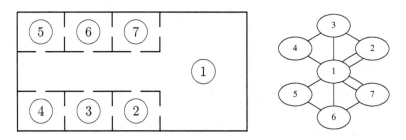

Figure 19.7.: Left: Floor plan of a museum with doors closed. Now there is an Euler circuit for this floor plan. Right: Graph representation of the floor plan.

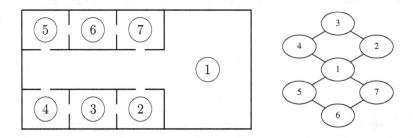

Definition 19.9. Hamilton Path

Let $g(v, e)$ be a graph with vertices v and edges e. The a **Hamiltonian Path** is a sequence of vertices that traverses each vertex precisely once. If the path starts and stops at the same vertex an visits every other vertex exactly once it is called an **Hamiltonian Circuit** or **Hamiltonian Cycle**

Of interest, say, for bicyclers or deliverymen are Hamiltonian circuits. A traveler would like to visit every node without back-tracking. Any Hamiltonian cycle can be converted to a Hamiltonian path by removing one edge from the path, but the reverse is not necessarily true unless the first and last node are adjacent.

Exercises

1. Suppose a graph $g(v, e)$ is represented by a quadrilateral with intersecting diagonals. Show how to redraw the graph so that it is planar.

2. Try to come up with examples of a graphs with 6, 7, 8, 9 and 10 nodes where every vertex has degree of at least 2 for which there is no Eulerian circuit.

3. Try to come up with examples of a graphs with 6, 7, 8, 9 and 10 nodes where every vertex has degree of at least 2 for which there is an Eulerian circuit and illustrate the circuit.

4. Try to come up with examples of a graphs with 6, 7, 8, 9 and 10 nodes where every vertex has degree of at least 2 for which there is no Hamiltonian circuit.

5. Try to come up with examples of a graphs with 6, 7, 8, 9 and 10 nodes where every vertex has degree of at least 2 for which there is a Hamiltonian circuit and illustrate the circuit. e root and the leaves.

6. Draw a binary tree with 11 nodes.

7. A polyhedral graph is a planar graph where the edges represent the edges of a polygon. Draw a polyhedral graph of a pyramid (square base and triangular sides).

8. Draw a polyhedral graph of a cube.

9. Draw a polyhedral graph of an octahedron.

10. A full binary tree is one in which every parent has precisely two children. Prove that every binary tree with n internal vertices (vertices that neither root nor leaf) has a total of $2n + 1$ vertices.

11. Prove that a full binary tree has a total of $n + 1$ terminal vertices.

12. Implement a directed graph class in Python. You should include operations to add, remove, and extract nodes. Each node should be able store data. Look in the course catalog for your college and populate the graph with all of the computer science courses. Add an edge for each each prerequisite. Implement an function **pathway(course)** that will return a graph of courses showing what must be taken prior to taking any other course.

13. Write a program to determine if a path is an Euler circuit. Use any graph implementation you like.

14. Write a program to determine if a path is an Hamilton circuit. Use any graph implementation you like.

15. Use **pygraphviz** or other visualization software to display the pathway for at least five advanced courses with multiple prerequisites. Each course should have at least one pre-requiste that is at least 2 edges away.

16. Extend the **tree** class defined in the text to build a family tree. At the minimum you will need to include a spousal pointer. Populate it with your (or another) family tree including some cousins, grandparents, siblings, and uncles or aunts.

17. Implement a tree traversal program in Python that will find the relationship between two individuals in a family tree.

20 . Decidability and Computability

When faced with a homework exercise every student wants to know, "How do I solve this problem?" Prerequisite to this is the question: "Does this problem have a solution?" Before attempting to solve a complicated problem it might be wise to determine if a solution even exists. In real life, the solutions are not cut and dry: diplomats may "decide," for example, that coexistence is incompatible with peace, or prosperity is incompatible with ecology. A math student might choose to look in the back of the book for answers. (Note that this book does not have answers the back, so there is no guarantee that solutions exist for all the problems in it!). For example, one can easily come up with may paradoxical questions. One of these if Russell's paradox: an element can be a subset of itself if and only if it is not a subset of itself (Bertrand Russell, 2018).

Theorem 20.1. Russell's Paradox

Let $S = \{x | x \notin x\}$. Then $S \in S \iff S \notin S$.

Proof. Let $S = \{x | x \notin x\}$

Proof of sufficiency: suppose $S \in S$. By the defining property of S any element of S is not in itself. Hence $S \notin S$. Hence we conclude that $S \in S \Rightarrow S \notin S$.

Proof of necessity: suppose that $S \notin S$. By the defining property of S, it is not true that $S \notin S$, i.e., it is true that $\neg(S \notin S)$. Hence $S \in \S$. We conclude that $S \notin S \Rightarrow S \in S$.

Taking the necessity and sufficiency together completes the proof, therefore $S \in S \iff S \notin S$. □

▶ ▶ ▶ **Example 20.1.** **Barber Paradox**. In a medieval town there lives a male barber who shaves all those men, and only those men, that do not shave themselves. Who shaves the barber?

Suppose the barber shaves himself. This is not possible, because the barber only shaves men that do not shave themselves.

Suppose somebody who is not the barber shaves the barber. This means the barber does not shave himself. Thus the barber must shave himself. This contradicts the previous paragraph.

Bertram Russell pointed out that the Barber Paradox, while in itself a paradox, is not precisely a restatement of Russell's paradox. Can you figure out what the difference is? ◄ ◄ ◄

Problems like these are said be **undecidable**: there is no correct answer. In 1928, David Hilbert challenged the mathematical world with his *Entscheidungsproblem* (**decidability problem**): Given any mathematical statement, is it possible to determine, using the axioms, theorems, and body of mathematical knowledge derived thereof, whether the statement is true or false.

Related to this is the question of whether the set of axioms on which mathematics relies is complete, i.e., are there enough axioms to derive the theorems and other results you need? Since paradoxes arise it seems that there is something inherently wrong with the underlying dependence of mathematics on formal logic.

Definition 20.1. Completeness

Let S be a set of axioms. Then we say S is complete if every statement X can be proven as either true or false from the axioms in S.

A set of basic axioms should be consistent in the sense that anything we derive from it should not lead to a contradiction. If would be something of a disaster if we were to able to prove contradictory statements, like "2 is an integer" and "2 is not an integer," because then we would not know what 2 was. This would ultimately invalidate our entire body of knowledge.

Definition 20.2. Consistency

Let S be a set of axioms. Then we say S is consistent if for all X, is not possible derive both X and $\neg X$ from S.

The **Halting Problem** is the equivalent formulation of the decidability problem in computer science: given any computer program P, is it possible to write another computer program Q that takes P as input and determine, in a finite amount of time, whether or not P will eventually halt (e.g., complete its complete is computation) or loop forever?

Theorem 20.2. Halting Problem

Then there does not exist any program H that takes as input a program P and its input data I and determines whether or P will eventually halt on input I or will loop forever on input I.

Proof. Prove by contradiction: assume that there is a program H that will make such a determination.

1. Since any program P might have some input I let us express H as $H(P, I)$.

2. Since H exists, for any input tuple (P, I), either

   a) $H(P, I)$ prints "Halts", if it determines that P will halt with input I; or else
   b) $H(P, I)$ prints "Loops Forever", if it determines that P will NOT halt with input I

3. Consider the notation $H(P, P)$. This is the output that is printed by H for the input tuple (P, P), namely, its determination of how P will behave with P as input. This notation is reasonable because we consider both P and I to be strings of text characters.

4. Construct a new computer program $K(P)$. The input to K is $H(P, P)$ and it will do exactly the opposite of what $H(P, P)$ tells it to do:

   a) $H(P, P)$ prints "Halts" $\iff$ $K(P)$ loops forever.
   b) $H(P, P)$ prints "Loops Forever" $\iff$ $K(P)$ halts.

5. Now consider what happens if we input K to K, i.e, what does $K(K)$ do?

a) According to step 4b, if $K(K)$ halts then $H(K, K)$ prints "loops forever", by the construction of K. But by the construction of H, if K halts with input K, according to step 2a, $H(K, K)$ will always print "halts". So we have a contradiction.

b) If $K(K)$ loops forever, then $H(K, K)$ prints "Halts", according to step 4a. But by the construction of H, if $K(K)$ loops forever, $H(K, K)$ prints "loops forever" (step 2b). This is also a contradiction.

□

One way to prove that a problem is undecidable is with the **method of reduction**: prove that problem X is equivalent to the Halting Problem. This would mean that you can solve X if and only if you can solve the Halting Problem. Since you can't solve the Halting problem, you can't solve X. Here are some examples of undecidable problems that are equivalent to the Halting Problem:

- **Totality Problem:** Will an arbitrary program enter halt on all inputs?

  Consequence: You can't write a program to find all the infinite loops in a program.

- **Equivalence Problem:** Will two computer programs compute the same output for every input?

  Consequence: there is no guarantee that you can find the most optimally efficient algorithm.

A generalization of the Halting Problem is given by Rice's theorem.

Theorem 20.3. Rice's Theorem

Only trivial properties of a computer program (equivalently, Turing Machine, or Computer Language) are decidable.

A non-trivial property (one that is not decidable) is one that (a) describes the general input/output behavior of the program; and (b) is a a property of some programs but not all programs, such as "the input to this program contains at least two different strings."

Theorem 20.4. Incompleteness Theorem (Gödel)

Any theory capable of expressing elementary arithmetic cannot be both consistent and complete. In particular, for any effective formal theory that proves certain mathematical facts, there is a statement that is **True** but cannot be prove in that theory. Such as statement is known as a **Gödel Sentence**.

▶ ▶ ▶ **Example 20.2.** **The Liar Paradox.** Consider the following statement:

P : This sentence is false.

If P is **True**, then by construction it is **False**; if P is **False**, then by construction it is **True**. A Gödel sentence similar to the Liar Paradox is

P : This sentence is not provable.

◀ ◀ ◀

Gödel's approach to the theory of decidability was to define a class of *general recursive functions*. This is a set of of recursively enumerable functions that is closed under arithmetical operations such as function composition. A set S is said to be **recursively enumerable** if there is some algorithm that can enumerate the members of the set. Gödel defined computability in terms of general recursion (definition 3).

Definition 20.3. Gödel's Postulate

A function is **computable** if and only if it is general recursive.

Church defined a mathematical notation called the **lambda calculus**. The `lambda` expressions in Python are based on expressions in the lambda calculus. These expressions are sometimes called pure functions, and can be used to define higher order mathematical structures. Church equated computability with the ability to express a function in the lambda calculus

---

(def 4). He then went on to prove that the decision problem cannot be solved using the lambda calculus (theorem 20.5).[1]

Definition 20.4. Churh's Computability Postulate

A function is computable if and only if it can be written in terms of the lambda calculus.

Theorem 20.5. Church's Theorem

The Decision Problem cannot be solved using Lambda Calculus.

The Turing Machine[2] is a conceptual machine that manipulates an infinitely long paper type. The machine can read or write the a single symbol (called the current symbol)on the tape. It can move the tape forwards or backwards one square at a time. A Turing Machine consists of the following components:

1. A tape, divided into cells. Each cell has either a one, a zero, or is blank.
2. A head that can read and write the current cell.
3. A mechanism to move the head forward or backward by one cell.
4. A state register that contains the state of the machine (the value of the current cell).
5. A table of instructions that tells the machine what do do, e.g, "if you read three 1's in a row moving left, move one step to the right and write a 0."

Turing that a function was computable if and only if an algorithm could be written to compute it on this machine.

---

[1] Alonzo Church (1936). Am. J. Mathematics, 58:345-363.
[2] Turing, A.M. (1936). Proc. London Math. Soc. 42: 230-265.

Definition 20.5. Turing Computable

A function is computable if and only if it can be computed by a Turing Machine.

Theorem 20.6. Turing's Theorem

The decision problem can not be solved using a Turing Machine.

It seemed for a while that Gödel, Church and Turing were taking different approaches, and that perhaps eventually somebody would stumble on the right approach, namely, one in which the decision problem could be solved. However, it turns out that all of these approaches are equivalent.

Theorem 20.7. Equivalence of Computing Models (Kleene, Church, Turing and Rosser)

The following definitions of computability are equivalent,
1. Gödel's recursive functions;
2. Church's λ-calculus;
3. Turing machines
in the sense that any statement that can be proven in one, can be proven in another; and any statement that cannot be prove in one, cannot be proven in any of the others. Any function that can be implemented using any of these methods is said to be **computable**.

The obvious problem for computer scientists is that one does not want to waste time writing programs to solve problems that can't be solved. What remains open here is whether any of these definitions of computability are relevant to them. For a programmer, a computable function is one that he or she can implement in a computer program, such that when the implementation is invoked, it produces the correct answer. Thus a function is computable if there exists an algorithm that can be effectively translated into good code. It needs to produce an valid answer within a reasonable about of time to any valid input.

Definition 20.6. Effective Algorithm

An **effective procedure** or **algorithm** is a sequence of steps that:
1. Always gives an answer.
2. Always gives a correct answer.
3. Always calculates the answer in a finite number of steps.
4. Always works for all instances of problems in the class.

A function that can be calculated with an effective procedure is called **effectively calculable**.

Proposition 20.8. Church-Turing Thesis

Every effectively calculable function is computable.

Proposition 20.8 is generally taken either as a definition or an axiom because it has not been proven. It is widely believed to be true however. If it is true, it means that not all problems can be solved by effective methods. But not all concepts of computation are bound by the Church-Turing Hypothesis. For example, there is no indication that the human brain can be fully represented by a Turing machine.

An **oracle machine**, for example, is a Turing Machine with a second tape that is read-only. Oracle machines can solve problems that are far more complex than Turing Machines, and can be shown to computer some funtions that cannot be computed but a Turing machine. An oracle machine that can solve the Halting problem for a Turing Machine is called a **hypercomputer**.

The Halting Problem still applies at each level of computation. Even though a hypercomputer can solve the Halting Problem for a Turing Machine, it cannot solve the Halting Problem for a hypercomputer. This has led to the concept of an **arithmetical hierarchy of hypercomputers**.

A **Stored-Program Computer** is a computer architecture (hardware design concept) in which the instructions are stored as a program or sequence of instructions in memory. The term is often used interchangeably with **von Neumann architecture** which is more specific, and refers a specific type of stored program computer consisting of a **central processing unit**

(CPU, a device that does computations) and a single memory storage entity that is used to store both programs and data. All modern computers are based on the von Neuman architecture. If the Church-Turing thesis is true, then the following proposition holds true.

> ### Proposition 20.9. Computability on von Neuman Architecture
>
> The von Neuman Architecture is Turing computable, i.e., a function can be computed on a Turing machine if and only if it can be computed in a Stored-Program Computer.

A. A Quick Tour of Python

This appendix provides a brief tour of Python. For more details the reader should consult the official documentation[1], notably, the *Tutorial*[2], the *Library Reference*[3], and the *Language Reference*.[4]

Distinguishing Python from the Crowd

Python is an open source, multi-paradigm language that has features common to many structured, object-oriented, procedural and functional programming languages. It is free[5] and code is platform independent. Python is maintained by the Python Software Federation; their web page at `http://www.python.org` is the first place to go for more details. Generic features and implicit typing make it easy to learn. For example, the traditional "Hello World!" program is reduced to a single line in Python:

```
print("Hello World!")
```

While the name Python is taken from the TV show *Monty Python's Flying Circus*, you do not have to like the show, "but it helps. :)"[6]

Python is more than just a computer language. Python code can be evaluated in several different ways:

- In the Python shell – this is a command line interface that allows users to evaluate single expressions (including function definitions, loops, etc) on the screen. The values of all identifiers are remembered until you close the session. There is a more advanced version of the shell call iPython.

- As Python scripts – these are programs that are stored in text files

---

[1]See `https://docs.python.org/3/index.html`.
[2]See `https://docs.python.org/3/tutorial/index.html`.
[3]See `https://docs.python.org/3/library/index.html`.
[4]See `https://docs.python.org/3/reference/index.html`.
[5]Free both in the sense of free beer and free speech.
[6]See `https://docs.python.org/2/faq/general.html#do-i-have-to-like monty-python-s-flying-circus`.

(e.g., like java or C code) and then executed from the command line. They are compiled to byte code before being executed. If a byte code file with the same name as your Python script already exists, the byte code file will be executed, unless the Python code is newer. If the Python code is newer than an existing byte code file with the same name, new byte code will be produced and executed.

- In a Jupyter notebook – these are like laboratory notebooks that combine the advantages of scripting and shells. You can intersperse blocks of text, code, and output. It has the advantage of the Python shell in that it keeps a record of everything that is done. It has the advantage of Python scripts but multiple long programs can be included in different blocks in the notebook. Each block knows about every other executable block that has been previously evaluated.

Most standard integrated development environments support Python, so if you are stuck on Eclipse or Vim, please continue your merry way. If not, a very simple IDE called idle[7] is bundled with Python.

Version 3 or Version 2?

When you install Python, you have two choices: Python 2 and Python 3. Both versions are currently being maintained but as time goes by, more people will be using version 3 and fewer are using version 2. If you are new to Python, it is best to start with Python 3; otherwise it you will have to upgrade (eventually, if not now). There are only a few differences between the two versions. As of the publication of this book, the latest versions were 2.7 and 3.6. Python 2.7 will be the last official release of Python 2. There are four principal differences:

- The syntax of **print** statements.
- Handling of integer division. In Python 3, the result of **5/2** is now **2.5**. In Python 2 the result was **2**. To force integer division in Python 3, you need to use the integer division operator **5//2**.
- The default string format is Unicode rather than ASCII
- Handling of most list operations such as **range**, **map**, etc. An explicit

---

[7]Named after Eric Idle, one of the actors in *Monty Python's Flying Circus*. There is another less popular IDE called eric, named after the same actor.

cast to **list** is neccessary to create a list out of the result, as a form of lazy evaluation is now used by default.

.

Where to Get Python Installers

Python can be written on Linux, Mac and Windows operating systems. All Python programs are platform independent; any Python program written on one operating systems (e.g., Windows) is completely transferable to another (e.g., Linux or MacOS), without modification.

Chances are that you already have some version of Python on your system. To find out, open and command window and type

```
python3 --version
```

If this gives an error message, then you do not have Python 3 installed.

The intricacies of setting up and using Python on different operating systems are detailed in the official documentation.[8] There are several ways to install Python.

1. The easiest way to install Python is to use Anaconda. This is a commercial development environment that is free for non-commercial users. Anaconda includes a dashboard, multiple development environments, and a GUI package manager as well as the standard Python libraries. Anaconda is available for Mac, Windows, and Linux.

2. You can download installers (or compile from source code) from `https://www.python.org`. You should probably only do this if you are already a more sophisticated programmer who has a preferred IDE that they want to use.

3. You can use a package manager to install Python on Linux systems. (Note for MacOs users: Python is generally incompatible with MacOS package managers like Brew.) This option is not available for

---

[8]See `https://docs.python.org/3/using/index.html`.

Windows users. Using your package manager is the preferred method of installation for all Linux users.

If you installed your software using methods 2 or 3 you can use the Python package manager **pip** for all subsequent Python library updates. If you used method 1 you should use the **conda** package manager.

Many users prefer to code in an IDE and run from the command line. Alternatively, you can download the Jupyter notebook interface.[9] Most new users find the notebook interface to be a lot easier as it allows you to contain programs, documentation, and output in one file, so that you can easily follow the work flow. Jupyter is included in Anaconda.

Identifiers

Identifiers (i.e., variable names) are case sensitive, and may contain any number of letters, numbers, and the underscore character. An identifier may not begin with an underscore. The following are distinct identifiers: **spam**, **Spam**, **SPAM**, and **_Spam**. Thus **_99_cent_Spam** is available but **99_Cent_Spam** is not.[10]

If you see something that looks like a period inside of an identifier (like in R) is really a library delimiter: **spam.eggs.bacon(2)** refers to the function **bacon** in the library **spam.eggs** or a class attribute.

Identifiers in your code must be different from Python keywords.

Table A.1. Python Keywords					
False	None	True	and	as	assert
break	class	continue	def	del	elif
else	except	finally	for	from	global
if	import	in	is	lambda	nonlocal
not	or	pass	raise	return	try
while	with	yield			

---

[9]See http://jupyter.readthedocs.io/en/latest/install.html#id2.

[10]While it is standard in most computer languages to use **foo**, **bar** and **foobar** as dummy variables, in Python the preferred silly variables are **spam**, **eggs**, and anything from *Monty Python's Flying Circus*.

Numeric Data: int, float, complex, boolean

You can determine the data type of an identify with the **type** function. The data type of an identifier is determined dynamically, when you assign a value to it. You can change the data type of an identifier by assigning value with a different type to it.

Numeric data types are integers (type **int**); floating point (type **float**); and complex (type **complex**). Standard mathematical operators can be used for multiplication (**A*B**); addition (**A+B**); subtraction (**A−B**); floating point division (**A/B**); integer division (**A//B**); remainder after division (**A%B**); negation (**−A**); and exponentiation (**A**B**). Parenthesis may be used to override order of operations. Complex numbers are written as in **3+4j**; if there is any space before the letter **j**, it will be treated as an identifier and not as $\sqrt{-1}$. The complex number $3 + i$ is written as **3+1j** and not as **3+j**.

Boolean operations may be performed on integer data types; these are performed bit by bit. There is a bitwise or function (**A|B**); a bitwise exclusive or that is sometimes confused with exponentiation (**A^B**); bitwise and (**A&B**); shift left and shift right (**A<<B** or **A>>B**); and bitwise negation (**~A**).

There is a Boolean data type that returns a value of **True** or **False**. Boolean variables may use the infix operators for and (**A and B**); or (**A or B**); and negation (**not A**). The results of testing for relatively equality, for example, in if or while statements, returns a values that can be combined this way.

Assignments

Assignments are written with a single equal sign, as in

```
x=3
y=5*x+23
```

Augmented assignments (such as **+=**, ***=**, **/=**, **−=**, ****=**, **%=**, etc.) combine arithmetic operations with assignment, such as

```
x+=17
```

which means "add 17 to the current value of **x** and store the result in **x**."

Suppose you want to swap the values of **x** and **y**. As soon as you set **x=y** you have two copies of **y** and have lost the original value of **x**. So what you normally do is save the value of one of the two variables in a temporary variable:

```
temp = x
x = y
y = temp
```

You can certainly still do this in Python. But there is an easier way. Because Python evaluates everything on the right hand side of the equal sign of an assignment *before* anything on the left hand side of the equal sign, you can do this instead:

```
x,y = y,x
```

Really you have a tuple on the left and a tuple on the right. The value of the tuple on the right is completely evaluated (and stored in a temporary location) before being assigned to anything. Then the items in the tuple are assigned, in sequence, to the variables listed on the left.

Table A.2. Operator Precedence

	Operator	Description
0. (Highest)	()	force order of evaluation
1.	**	exponentiation
2.	~,+, -	unary plus, minus
3.	*, /, %, //	multiplication, division
4.	+, -	addition, subtraction
5.	>>, <<	bit shift
6.	&	bitwise and
7.	|, ^	bitwise or/xor
8.	<, >, <=, >=	compare
9.	==, !=, <>	test equal/not equal
10.	=, +=, -=, %=, /=, //=, *=, **=	augmented assign
11.	is, is not	identity
12.	in, not in	membership
13. (Lowest)	not, or, and	logical

Assignments to Boolean variables may include tests for equality:

```
x,y,z=17,20,17
p=(x==y)
q=(x==z)
r=(y==z)
p,q,r
```

```
(False, True, False)
```

```
(x<y,x>=z,x==z)
```

```
(True, True, True)
```

Sequential Data: lists, tuples, strings, range

Sequential data types of most interest to students include **lists**, **tuples**, **ranges**, and **strings**. Sequential objects may be accessed by index, starting with zero. Sequential data types are either **mutable** or **immutable**. Mutable data types may be changed, e.g., by reassignment of values, concatenation, or item deletion. Immutable objects may not be changed.

- A `list` is enclosed in square brackets. Lists may contain other lists, as well as any other Python data object:

  ```
  breakfast_items=[spam, eggs, cereal, oatmeal]
  dessert=[cookies,strawberries]
  food=breakfast+dessert
  someOddNumbers=[1,3,5,7,9,43]
  del someOddNumbers[2]
  print(food)
  print(someOddNumbers)
  ```

  ```
  [spam, eggs, cereal, oatmeal, cookies, dessert]
  [1, 3, 7, 9, 43]
  ```

- Tuples are immutable sequences normally enclosed in parenthesis. However, the parenthesis can be omitted when there is no ambiguity.

  ```
  squares=(4**2,5**2,6**2)
  print(squares[1])
  ```

25

```
a,b,c=squares
print(b)
```

25

- Strings are mutable sequences of characters, and are delimited by quotes (either single or double).

```
breakfast="egg-&-"
lunch="spam-&-"
food=3*(breakfast+lunch)
print(food)
```

egg-&-spam-&-egg-&-spam-&-egg-&-spam-&-

- A **range** sequence is used to represent a sequence of integers at fixed integers. Normally **range**'s are used for iteration through loops. To save storage space, only the first and last integer and the step size are actually stored; the values are not determined until the **range** is evaluated. To print out the values, for example, you must explicitly cast the **range** as a **list**. Students familiar with Python 2.7 will recognize this as the old **xrange** function, which no longer exists in Python 3.

```
list(range(5))
```

```
[0, 1, 2, 3, 4]
```

```
list(range(5,10))
```

```
[5, 6, 7, 8, 9]
```

```
list(range(5,32,5))
```

```
[5, 10, 15, 20, 25, 30]
```

Table A.3. Common Operations on Sequential Data Types

Example	Result and Description
`[5,6,7,8,9][:3]`	`[5,6,7]` – Leading items of list. Specifies number of items to return.
`[5,6,7,8,9][3:]`	`[8,9]` – Items at end of list to return. Specifies starting index.
`[5,6,7,8,9][2:4]`	`[7,8]` – List starting at first index up to but not including second index.
`7 in [5,6,7,8,9]`	`True` – membership in a sequence
`7 not in [5,6,7,8,9]`	`False`
`4 in [5,6,7,8,9]`	`False`
`4 not in [5,6,7,8,9]`	`True`
`[1,2]+[5,8]`	`[1,2,5,8]` – sequence concatenation
`"hi" + "world"`	`"hiworld"`
`3*[1,2]`	`[1,2,1,2,1,2]` – sequence repetition
`3*"--hello--"`	`"--hello----hello----hello''`
`max([5,6,7])`	`7` – largest item in the sequence
`min("cat`	`"a"` – smallest item in the sequence
`len([5,6,7])`	`3` – length of the sequence

Sets

Sets are collections of items enclosed in curly brackets. You can assign items to a set in an assignment statement. The order of items is not important, and duplicates are ignored:

```
S={1,2,3,4,2,1}
S
```

```
{1,2,3,4}
```

Because the order of elements does not matter, set elements may not be accessed by index. If a list is cast as set, then any duplicate elements will be lost. The empty set is assigned as **S=set()** and may not be assigned by using an empty pair of curly brackets (this avoids any ambiguity with a dictionary).

Standard set operations such as union (**S|T**), intersection (**S&T**), and set difference (**S-T**) can be performed on set variables. Augmented assigment

---

is also allowed with these operators. The expression **x in S** returns **True** when **x** is a member of **S**, and **False** otherwise.

Dictionaries

Dictionaries are content-addressable data collections stored as **key:value** pairs separated by commas and enclosed in curly brackets. An empty dictionary is assigned as **D={}**. For example,

```
ages={"tom":10, "dick":11, "harry":9}
ages["dick"]
```

```
11
```

An error occurs if an inquiry is made for a key that is not in the dictionary. To prevent this error you first check to see if it is there. The expression **"dick" in D** will return **True** if there is a key whose value is equal to **"dick"**, and it will return **False** otherwise. You can also obtain a list of all the keys in the dictionary as a list

```
list(ages.keys())
```

```
['tom', 'harry', 'dick']
```

Note that the order in which the keys are returned is not necessarily either the order in which they were assigned or lexicographical order.

Dictionaries can contain any Python object as values, even other dictionaries. A dictionary may even be heterogeneous:

```
{'tom': 1,
 'harry': {'phone': '555-1212', 'age': 42},
 'dick': [5, 10, 15]}
```

Tests and Loops

Python contains one test statement, **if**, and two types of loops: **for** and **while**. Under certain conditions, each of these statements tell Python to

---

execute a block of code. In the Python documentation, a block of code is called a **suite**.

Each suite must follow the following rules:

- The line of code immediately prior to the suite must end in a colon character(`:`).
- Every line in the suite is indented at least one space from the line ending with the colon.
- Every line in the suite must be indented the same number of spaces (except for nested loops or nests **if**'s).
- The line of code immediately after the last line of the suite must be dedented back to (realigned with) the same column that the line ending in the colon started in.

The **if** statement looks something like this:

```
if x<180:
    y=math.sin(x)
    z=math.cos(x)
    print(x, y, z)
print("I am all done printing!")
```

The suite of statements that assigns values to **y** and **z**, and then prints **x**, **y**, and **z** is only executed if the test **x<180** evaluates to **True**. If it does not evaluate to true the entire suite is ignored and the line "I am all done printing!" is the only thing that will be printed.

The **if** statement has an either/or option called **if..else**, illustrated here:

```
if b**2 < 4*a*c:
    print("There are no real roots.")
else:
    print("There are real real roots.")
```

Finally, we can include an **elif** (meaning "else if") clause in the middle:

```
if b**2 > 4*a*c:
    print("There are two real roots.")
elif b**2 == 4*a*c:
    print("There is a real, repeated root.")
else:
    print("The roots are a complex conjugate pair.")
```

When the **elif** statement is used, the **else** part of the statement becomes optional. Furthermore, multiple **elif** may be lined up in a row, one after another. Here is an encoding of an imaginary graduated tax table.

```
if income < 10000.0:
    tax = 0
elif income < 20000.0:
    tax = 0.10*(income-10000.0)
elif income < 30000.0:
    tax = 1000.0 + 0.15 * (income-20000.0)
elif income < 40000.0:
    tax = 2500.0 + 0.20 * (income-30000.0)
elif income < 50000.0:
    tax = 4500.0 + 0.25 * (income-40000.0)
else:
    tax = 7000.0 + 0.30 * (income-50000.0)
```

The **while** loop repeats a suite for as long as a test is true. The test is done before entry to the loop. If the test is true, the suite is executed. Then the test is performed again; if it remains true, the suite is executed again, and so on.

```
n=10;
nfact=1
j=1
while j<=n:
    nfact*=j
    j+=1
print("10!=",nfact)
```

```
10! = 3628800
```

A **for** loop is used to iterate over elements of a sequence such as a list.

```
nfact=1
for j in range(1,11):
    nfact*=j
print("10! =",nfact)
```

```
10! = 3628800
```

Comprehension

Python comprehensions are ways of encoding the mathematical expression $\{f(x)|x \in S\}$, where f is some function or and S is some domain. There are three types of comprehensions: list comprehension, set comprehension, and generator comprehension. These are one-line expressions that produce lists, sets, and generators, respectively. For example, to produce a list of the squares of the first ten positive integers, use **list comprehension**:

```
[x**2 for x in range(1,11)]
```

```
[1, 4, 9, 16, 25, 36, 49, 64, 81, 100]
```

You can specify for complicated domains. For example, to produce a list that encodes the set of tuples

$$\{(x, x^2, x^3)|(1 \leqslant x \leqslant 10) \wedge (x \text{ is even})\}$$

```
[(x, x**2, x**3) for x in range(1,11) if x%2==0]
```

```
[(2, 4, 8), (4, 16, 64), (6, 36, 216), (8, 64, 512),
(10, 100, 1000)]
```

Set comprehension works the same way as list comprehension; you just enclose the comprehension in curly braces rather than square braces, and the result is a set instead of a list.

```
{(x, x**2, x**3) for x in range(1,11) if x%2==0}
```

```
{(2, 4, 8), (4, 16, 64), (6, 36, 216), (8, 64, 512),
(10, 100, 1000)}
```

Since sets ignore duplicates, the results may not be quite the so similar. For example, the following gives a list of the remainders after computing 0/3, 1/3, 2/3, ..., 9/9.

```
[j%3 for j in range(10)]
```

```
[0, 1, 2, 0, 1, 2, 0, 1, 2, 0]
```

If we compute the results as a set, we are asking for the set of all possible remainders in the sequence 0/3, 1/3, 2/3, ..., 9/3. In as set, the duplicates are ignored:

```
{j%3 for j in range(10)}
```

```
{0, 1, 2}
```

We get a generator comprehension if the expression is enclosed in parenthesis. This is a one-line shorthand for a generator expression.

```
(x**3 for x in range(1,10))
```

```
<generator object <genexpr> at 0x7f65b4371ba0>
```

A generator is a sequence that uses lazy evaluation, i.e., the elements of the sequence are not actually calculated until they are needed. Generators can be used, for example, as the argument of a for statement, without actually storing the entire list. Suppose you want to print all the cubes that are under 1000 but don't know where to stop. You can be silly an use a really big generator, but stop when you get to 1000. (Of course this is silly because we would never want to go to $x = 10,000,000$ if we want to stop when $x^3 = 1000$.) The point is that the the ten million integers in the following example are never actually calculated nor stored.

```
u=(x**3 for x in range(1, 10000000))
for j in u:
    if j<1000:
        print(j)
    else:
        breaku=(x**3 for x in range(1, 10000000))
for j in u:
    if j<1000:
        print(j, end=" ")
    else:
        break
```

```
1 8 27 64 125 216 343 512 729
```

A **break** will exit the nearest enclosing **for** or **while** loop. In this case, as soon as we reach a cube that exceeds 1000, we break the **for** loop.

The **end=" "** in the **print** statement tells Python what to do after printing. Normally Python adds a newline character to what it prints. Here we told it to print a blank space instead. This means that the next thing printed comes out on the same line.

Functions

A function in Python is defined starting with a **def** statement and contain a single suite of code. A single object may be returned; multiple items can be returned as a tuple, by enclosing the results in parenthesis. The return value is specified with the **return** statement. If there is no **return** statement in the function then no value is returned when the function is invoked.

```
def AddUsUp(x,y,z):
    theSum=x+y+z
    return(theSum)

AddUsUp(5,10,17)
```

```
32
```

Normally you would explicitly specify each argument. You can also unpack a list or tuple using the **splat** operator (*). In this example, the splat maps 3 to **x**, 6 to **y**, and 9 to **z**.

```
z=(3,6,9)
AddUsUp(*z)
```

```
18
```

Function parameters may have default values. In the function definition, all required parameters (those without default values) must be listed first. Default values are specified with equal signs.

```
def spammer(s,repeats=5):
    for j in range(repeats):
        print(s)
```

If you do not specify the optional parameters, then the default values are used.

```
spammer("I would like to plant a shrubbery!")
```

```
I would like to plant a shrubbery!
I would like to plant a shrubbery!
I would like to plant a shrubbery!
I would like to plant a shrubbery!
I would like to plant a shrubbery!
```

If you specify the values of the optional parameters, then the value you use overrides the default value.

```
spammer("I like onions!", repeats=3)
```

```
I like onions!
I like onions!
I like onions!
```

Map, Filter and Reduce

The **map** function applies a function to every element of a list. It returns a generator, so so to actually print it out you need to explicitly cast it as a list. Schematically, **map(f, [x0,x1,x2,...])** produces **[f(x0), f(x1), f(x2), ...]**.

Suppose we define a function **SquareMe** that returns the square of a number:

```
def SquareMe(x):
    return x**2
```

Then we can produce a list of the squares of the first ten integers with

```
list(map(SquareMe, range(1,11)))
```

```
[1, 4, 9, 16, 25, 36, 49, 64, 81, 100]
```

Maps are frequently used with lambda functions to avoid the need to define a function that will only be used once. A **lambda** function is a function without a name. The equivalent lambda definition of **SquareMe** is

```
lambda x:x**2
```

```
<function __main__.<lambda>>
```

We could have defined **SquareMe** as

```
SquareMe=lambda x:x**2
```

but there would not have really been any point to that. In connection with the **map**, however, we can use the **lambda** definition directly:

```
list(map(lambda x:x**2, range(1,11)))
```

This produces the exact same results, eliminating the need to define a function that is only needed once.

The **filter** function is similar to **map** but instead of returning the result of the evaluation, it picks the elements in the list for which the function is true. Thus **filter(f, u)** returns all those elements **x** in **u** for which **f(x)** is true.

We can define a **lambda** function that determines if an integer is even by

```
lambda x:x%2==0
```

If **x** is even, then **x%2==0** is **True**, and if **x** is odd, then **x%2==0** is **False**. So here we produce a list of the even squares of integers under 100.

```
u=[x**2 for x in range(1,11)]
list(filter(lambda x:x%2==0, u))
```

```
[4, 16, 36, 64, 100]
```

The **reduce** function recursively applies a function to a list. Given a list $[x_0, x_1, x_2, \dots]$ it first calculates the sequence

$$y_0 = f(x_0, x_1)$$
$$y_1 = f(y_0, x_2) = f(f(x_0, x_1), x_2)$$
$$y_2 = f(y_1, x_3) = f(f(f(x_0, x_1), x_2), x_3)$$

$$\vdots$$

For example, if we define $f(x, y) = x + y^2$, this will accrue $\sum x_i^2$.

```
from itertools import reduce
reduce(lambda x,y:x+y**2, range(1,11))
```

```
385
```

We can verify that this is correct using traditional summing:

```
sum([x**2 for x in range(1,11)])
```

```
385
```

Class Definitions

A class definition must include a institutionalization method (always called **__init__** and whatever other methods you need for your class to work. You cannot actually print out the class unless you expressly define a method that defines how to print it (for example, define a **__repr__** method.

The first argument of every class method refers to the actual object instantiated. By convention this is called **self**. When you invoke the method, you do not expressly refer to this argument. For example, we can define a two-dimensional vector class that includes methods for vector length and vector dot product.

```
class vector():
    def __init__(self, x, y):
        self.x = x
        self.y = y
    def length(self):
        from math import hypot as mathhypot
        return mathhypot(self.x, self.y)
    def dot(self,other):
        x1=self.x; y1=self.y
        x2=other.x; y2=other.y
        return x1*x2 + y1*y2
    def __repr__(self):
        return str("Vector("+str(self.x)+","+str(self.y)+")")
```

To instantiate the class, we can create two vectors **a** and **b**. The print statement only works because we have defined a **__repr__** method, which tells Python how to convert the class into a string for printing.

```
a=vector(1,3)
b=vector(5,7)
print(a, b)
```

```
Vector(1,3) Vector(5,7)
```

To get the dot product,

```
a.dot(b)
```

```
26
```

To find the lengths,

```
a.length(), b.length()
```

```
(3.1622776601683795, 8.602325267042627)
```

Index

www.ingramcontent.com/pod-product-compliance
Lightning Source LLC
La Vergne TN
LVHW081341050326
832903LV00024B/1245

* 9 7 8 1 7 2 0 4 0 5 9 7 9 *